D1395087

Victoria Leatham takes us into the world of self-harming behaviours, one that can be occupied by princesses to poor university students. Cutting oneself to draw blood is a scary and scarifying act, generally driven by guilt, but often associated with tension reduction and a buzz, and thus potentially addictive. Psychiatrists recognise that Bipolar Mood Disorder can present atypically for a few years – via eating, obsessive and self-injurious behaviours – before settling into a more orthodox pattern. Leatham moves beyond such scratching of the diagnostic surface to superbly reveal the inner perturbation and some of the multiple determinants of such behaviours.

Professor Gordon Parker
Executive Director, Black Dog Institute

Bloodletting

Bloodletting

VICTORIA LEATHAM

First published in Great Britain in 2005 by
Allison & Busby Limited
Bon Marche Centre
241-251 Ferndale Road
London SW9 8BJ
http://www.allisonandbusby.com

Copyright © 2004 by VICTORIA LEATHAM

The moral right of the author has been asserted.

This book is sold subject to the conditions that it shall not,
by way of trade or otherwise, be lent, resold, hired out or
otherwise circulated without the publisher's prior
written consent in any form of binding or cover other than
that in which it is published and without a similar condition
being imposed upon the subsequent
purchaser.

A catalogue record for this book is available from
the British Library.

10 9 8 7 6 5 4 3 2 1

ISBN 0 7490 8372 7

Printed and bound in the UK

To L and M.

There are always other options, even when it seems
like there aren't.

bloodletting n.

1. phlebotomy, the act or process of letting blood or bleeding, as by opening a vein or artery

2. outmoded medical practice used as a cure for illnesses ranging from fevers to hysteria

Have you ever had a lyric from a really crappy song or advertising jingle get stuck in your head? Something that just won't go away, no matter how much you don't want it to be there?

Imagine if, instead of a silly piece of music, it was an image. Imagine that image was something you found disturbing; say, rivers of rich burgundy blood gushing from slashes in your forearms.

What if, instead of this being a fleeting, irritating image, it took hold in your mind. It would be there on waking, it would push itself into your thoughts while you were watching television, driving, sitting at your desk. What if, gradually, your mind became your own personal continuously screening horror movie, starring yourself.

What would you do? Would you feel compelled to act on these thoughts? Do you think, if you did, it would help? Would you think yourself mad?

Would you tell anyone?

Prologue

Starving, binge-drinking and promiscuity are, for many people, just part of growing up. They were for me. I didn't do them all at once. The starving came first and the other two followed, several years later, when I finally managed to convince myself that the calories in alcohol didn't count.

> Parents don't like any of these things.
> But there are things they like even less.

When I was fifteen, hadn't had my period for six months and was unable to stand up without seeing stars, my mother took me to the doctor. It wasn't that she thought I was too thin – teenage girls diet after all – but that she was worried I was anaemic. I wasn't. According to our helpful family doctor, I would be just fine if only I ate more.

My mother and I drove home relieved, and life continued as before. I exercised, didn't eat anything that contained fat, butter, milk or sugar, and kept to myself. My mother and older brother argued; my father worked. I did my best not to upset anyone and studied hard.

I was polite to everyone.

It wasn't until eighteen months later, after I'd had my wisdom teeth out, and was standing in front of the bathroom mirror, that I realised I wasn't fine. My collarbones stood out, my skin was greeny-grey, and it was difficult to stand up straight. I needed to eat.

Many months after that, by which time I'd finished school and had had a year overseas, I was able to have a piece of cake without then needing to exercise. I was at university by then, and everyone was eating. It was normal, and it was fun.

Of course, there was a price to pay. Suddenly, I wasn't the perfect child anymore. Out of the house at last, I was behaving badly and enjoying it. My grades slipped, my thighs grew and I didn't ring home.

My mother was horrified. Hadn't they brought me up properly? Didn't I care? Didn't I have any respect for them? I even ignored the most important of the house rules, number three: 'smile before you speak'. Did I not care what other people thought? How other people felt? What had happened to me?

What had happened? I was growing up, that was all. It wasn't so very complicated.

The real problems hadn't even started. They didn't start until after I'd finished uni and had been dragged to the doctor one afternoon. I explained the problem: I wasn't happy. I was tired, I was listless, I lacked concentration, I wanted to sleep all the time and, and, and. I didn't need to say anything else. She prescribed Prothiaden, an antidepressant.

It wasn't the answer

Chapter One

I had no idea that the simple act of running a sharp blade across my wrist would change everything so completely.

I couldn't pretend anymore and I didn't care. I sat on the kitchen floor of Helen's house and cried. I knew that I was crossing a line. If I used a knife against myself then I would have transgressed to such an extent that everything else I did, and was ashamed about, would fall away to nothing. I'd be outside the normal social boundaries, in a place where the rules no longer applied. The idea, while frightening, was also extremely seductive – it would mean a sort of freedom.

I wasn't after happiness anymore. I just wanted to survive.

Though I'd toyed with the idea of cutting myself before, I never seriously thought I'd be able to do it. It goes against nature. It goes against that primal self-preservation instinct. If you accidentally brush up against a hot iron you don't leave your arm there. You move it away, as quickly as possible, and you rush to put ice on the burn to numb the pain. But that very pain can bring relief.

Relief was what I was looking for that day, and I didn't care how I got it. What I wanted – what I needed – was a pain that I could see and deal with. I couldn't cope with the mess inside me any longer and cutting myself seemed to be the best solution. I knew that it would work. What I didn't know was that I was about to engage in a behaviour that was not just dangerous but highly, highly addictive.

I knew I needed help. I had left five or six messages for Alex. He didn't want to be involved with me any longer, but I was desperate. I didn't know who else to call; no-one else knew what I was going through. I didn't believe he was out – he was just screening his calls. So I kept ringing. Sooner or later he'd have to pick up. I thought it would help just to hear his voice.

Finally he answered. He sounded annoyed. 'What do you want, Vic?'

'I just wondered if you wanted to do something later. Maybe I could come over?' I was pleading with him. If we saw each other and talked, maybe, maybe, things would improve.

'No, I don't think that's a good idea.'

'Why?'

'Basically, I don't want to see you. Not today. Not at all. I've got my own problems, I don't need you adding to them. Don't call me again. And don't expect me to change my mind and call you. I won't. In fact – and I wasn't going to tell you this, but it's probably better that you know – I destroyed your phone number last night.'

And that was pretty much it, really.

Spending time with Alex had undoubtedly been making matters worse, but I was addicted to his attention – albeit sporadic – and at least when with him I wasn't alone. We'd known each other for years and had kept in touch as we'd got older, sleeping with each other from time to time, but not having a relationship. He had the kind of Nordic looks that are hard to ignore: grandmothers loved him and gay waiters drooled over him. But underneath the angelic features and charm, there was an angry, aggressive intelligence and intolerant, dismissive attitude toward most people.

Alex had never pretended to love me, or even care about me, but nevertheless he wanted me. Not when he was sober of course; if I touched him then, he'd flinch. It was when he was drunk, or stoned, or high, that I was of interest. This was enough for me.

A week or so previously, we'd been drinking and had done a line or two of speed. It was summer. The temperature was over 35°C in Sydney's inner west and it was stifling inside his house. It seemed like the only relief we'd get would be in the ocean, so I let him drive my car through the city and across to Bronte Beach. Neither of us thought twice about the fact that we were under the influence. The influences, plural. Not only did we think we were indestructible, but we didn't care about the rest of the world.

We parked and walked down to the beach which, while pretty and sheltered, has notoriously strong surf. This afternoon was no exception. Normally, I'm scared of large waves and either go in when it's flat or just paddle at the shoreline. On this day and in that state, however, nothing worried me and I simply dived in. Alex was a strong swimmer, so didn't think twice.

We both swam beyond the breakers, he easily and me with some difficulty. For a few minutes we bobbed about looking back at the beach, physically tired but elated and refreshed.

Then, all too quickly, we found ourselves caught in a rip. We were being pushed toward the rocks. I tried to grab hold and haul myself onto them between the surges of the crashing waves. Ahead of me, Alex managed to do just this.

But it wasn't as easy as it looked, as the rocks were slippery. I couldn't get a hold, so was repeatedly thrown against them, and then dragged back into the ocean. After what might have only been a few minutes, I gave up. I just couldn't do it. The alcohol and drugs made drowning seem like a reasonable response, so I relaxed and calmly accepted my fate.

And then I felt someone grabbing my arms. I was back on the rocks, being dragged across them by Alex. He glared at me, annoyed that he'd had to help at all. I had drawn attention to us, and he'd ripped his knee open. I saw blood oozing from under a flap of white skin. Upset, bruised and scratched, I was otherwise unhurt. But it hadn't helped things between us – he couldn't even look at me as we walked up to the car.

As we drove home, now cold and sober, it appeared that Alex actively hated me. Perhaps this should have upset me; it didn't. Instead it seemed a natural and fair reaction. After all, I hated me too.

Alex wasn't an ideal companion perhaps, but he understood me. Now he'd gone I had to cope alone.

The idea of cutting myself had first occurred to me the previous year. I'd had yet another argument with my mother and was feeling guilty and inadequate. I was also very angry – with both her and myself. As I drove into town afterwards, sobbing so hard at times that I had to pull over to the side of the road, I remembered the knife on the kitchen bench. What if? I thought. I imagined cutting my wrist, and as I did so, I began to feel calmer. I even smiled to myself. Not that I'd ever do it, of course.

That image came back to me as I sat on the floor at Helen's house. I had to try it. Normally I would have been at college but I had a few days off. Helen was at work. Outside, it was sunny and warm. Somehow that made it even worse. Made everything much worse.

What I wanted was a simple response. I didn't want to feel, that was too difficult. I wanted to hurt, I wanted real, tangible, physical pain. That I could understand.

I stood up, and there it was. The breadknife. It was lying on the sink, inviting me to pick it up. As I looked at it, my stomach muscles tensed. I was still crying but now it was for a different reason. I knew that once I'd done this, I wouldn't be able to go back.

I reached out, and then held it for a minute above my wrist. My hand was shaking. This wasn't something I should be doing. This was not a good idea. But I'd started the process, and, I told myself, I had to follow it through. I tried to think clearly. How hard did I have to press so as to draw blood but not hit an artery? Was it easy to hit an artery? What if I did? What if I accidentally went too deep?

Then I'd deal with it, I told myself calmly. I was going to be fine.

Gritting my teeth, I put my forearm on the bench and quickly ran the blade across it, pressing as I did so.

There. It was over. It was done.

The tension lifted instantly, and I focused on what I had to do next. I wiped down the bench with a dish cloth, found a towel in the bathroom to wrap around my arm, and set off towards the nearest doctor's surgery.

I left the cloth scrunched up on the kitchen bench.

It wouldn't be fair to suggest that my flatmate Helen was unpleasant. She wasn't. On the contrary, she specialised in nice, neat and clean. Surrounded in a cloud of smug contentment, she was well groomed and well behaved. She'd smile sweetly at me in the mornings, and be polite to my friends. Still, she made it clear that this was her house, I was a lodger, and she didn't approve of me. This wasn't about Helen, but by leaving evidence lying around, I involved her. I don't know what I wanted her to do.

So, my wrist wrapped in a not-so-white-anymore towel, I walked across the park to the university medical centre. I felt – and this took me by surprise – exhilarated. My blood was pumping and I had energy. The grass looked greener than usual, and the sky bluer. There were ducks in the pond.

The doctor, who I'd seen before, didn't criticise me or ask me why I'd done it. Instead, as she was injecting the area with a local anaesthetic – which seemed ironic in the circumstances – and carefully sewing up the wound, she simply told me not to do it again. I should come back to see her if I felt I wanted to and, even if that meant coming in daily for a while, that was fine. As I left, she told me it wasn't a good habit to get into – and that it wasn't something likely to impress a future mother-in-law.

I laughed. I couldn't imagine anyone would ever want to marry me. 'No, I won't do it again,' I told her.

When I got home, the house was quiet and the dish cloth was gone. And I felt better. Much better. My wrist hurt, but not badly. It was more a low-grade ache than a sharp pain, just enough to remind me of what I'd done. The bandage was another reminder. For the first time in months, I felt together. Sharp. In hurting myself I had at last found a way to release the pressure.

But it was more than that. I was now different. I felt different. I'd discovered a way to control my feelings. Just because self-mutilation wasn't deemed 'an acceptable coping mechanism' didn't mean I was going to stop doing it.

Over the next few days Helen and I saw a bit of each other but she didn't refer to the incident. I thought this was a good thing until she came in to the kitchen as I was having breakfast one morning and told me to leave. It just wasn't working.

It hadn't been a good week, but now I had become someone my parents could really be ashamed of, someone who'd done something that was so far from their experience, and so outside their range of understanding, that they couldn't even talk about it. In some ways, I wasn't unhappy about this.

Chapter Two

Sitting halfway up the stairs in my new flat above the flower shop, I did something I never thought I'd do. I opened the phone book and looked up the number of a helpline. I'd always thought they were for those without friends, desperate teenagers living on the streets, lonely old alcoholics. I didn't think they were for people like me, people who were normal.

I dialled the number and a man answered.

I wasn't sure what to do next. Suddenly I didn't want to speak to him. Perhaps if a female had answered, it would have helped. 'What's your name?' he asked.

Maria? Anna? I wondered. But why bother pretending I was someone else to him? 'Vic,' I said.

'And what's the problem, Vic?' He sounded patronising. I hesitated. I didn't want to tell him but I needed to tell someone. 'I want to cut myself.' I'd held off doing anything since the first incident, but that didn't mean I'd lost the desire. I wanted to do it. I could visualise myself downstairs in the kitchen doing it, but thinking about it didn't give me relief now. It just tormented me. Nevertheless, I'd decided that cutting was something that should only be done in emergencies – it wasn't something I should do to relieve everyday stresses, no matter how tempting. But not doing it was proving very difficult. Very difficult.

'Well, that's not very good, is it? Why do you want to do something like that, Vic?'

The answer was obvious. 'I'd feel better.'

'So what is it that you feel bad about?'

I couldn't tell him, and instead hung up. I bit the inside of my lip so as not to cry. I just couldn't talk about this.

The bloke I was sharing with was nice enough. His major complaint about his last flatmate was that she watched too much TV and that she seemed to suffer from chronic fatigue syndrome. I should have taken notice of the way he said 'seemed'. He obviously didn't believe her.

Initially we got on pretty well. We shared meals from time to time, went to the pub together on the odd occasion to play pool, and drank beer on the balcony while watching the sun set over the surrounding houses, ignoring the trucks as they went by on the road below. Rodney's major flaws were a love of science fiction and a chip on his shoulder caused by the way other people reacted to his love of science fiction. They all felt he should have grown out of it. He hadn't but was in the process of reinventing himself in other ways.

He'd moved interstate, started a new job and was trying to shed his geek image. He now dressed like many others in Newtown pubs, in faded Levis and funky T-shirts with messages. He wore a leather thong around his neck, and his hair was slightly longish and tousled in a way that suggested he'd spent money on the cut, and he had recently taken up vegetarianism (not as a cause, I suspected, but as a fashion statement). He'd advertised the room in his art deco flat by putting up a card at a local café.

When I turned up to meet him, Rodney was friendly, open and very excited about what Sydney had to offer. I needed to live somewhere, so I played along with his enthusiasm, talking about films, and music, and the essay I was writing on transgression. Dressed in a denim miniskirt, Blundstone boots and a loud orange and green (long-sleeved) shirt with stylised naked women with big hair, I looked, and sounded, like the kind of flatmate he was after.

I was studying at art school, as after having completed an English degree, I'd decided I wasn't ready for the workforce. It took less than a month to work out that it was the wrong place for me. It wasn't like doing a casual drawing course or photography course. It was serious; the students were serious. Even when I had signed up, I'd been unsure, so was also studying for a Master's degree in English two evenings a week. It meant that I was very busy but I didn't see that as a problem. I saw it as a good thing: I'd taken the previous year off and was now ready to work hard. Besides, I didn't believe being busy could actually do any harm.

I told Rodney about one of the first exercises we did at college. It involved sound and performance. I sat on the floor cross-legged in a darkened room and watched as three of my classmates stood on a makeshift stage and made sounds with carrots.

Rhythmically, they chewed them, they chopped them and they blended them.

He laughed and decided on the spot that I'd be someone who'd be fun to live with. I was offered the room.

At the start, I was on my best behaviour and careful not to let him see my arm. I went to uni, wrote my essays, and worked at the weekends in the state gallery shop. I wasn't seeing my friends – as I'd become more miserable there seemed little point – and my relationship with my parents wasn't good, but I was coping. It was enough.

Then Alex contacted me. As he'd been the one to call, not me, I felt on surer ground. He really did want to see me. Not that either of us had changed. The time we spent together was as stifling, stressful and tense as it had always been.

We drank together and we slept together. Not that the latter was much fun, due largely to the Prothiaden, the antidepressant I was still taking. It didn't cheer me up, but did make me tired, listless, and not at all interested in sex.

Gradually, over the next few months, things deteriorated. I found myself staying in bed until 5 pm, only getting up so that Rodney wouldn't know. The numbness and lethargy were almost worse than the intense guilt I experienced as a result of not being able to function.

I moved around in a haze, finally dropping out of art school. I didn't say goodbye to anyone and no-one had my phone number.

My doctor, who really did try to help, explained that depression, along with affecting your mood, often meant that simple things became difficult. I didn't believe her. Instead I was angry with myself for being tired all the time, angry that walking up the street to do the shopping had become a trial, angry that I couldn't drive to Canberra – which was just three hours away – without stopping every half-hour for a rest. I was angry that I couldn't understand things I knew I could do. I really believed that if only I tried harder, it would all be fine. I felt it was my fault: I might be suffering from 'depression' but that didn't mean I couldn't will myself out of it.

I was still just able to write the essays I was required to do for my Master's degree. They didn't involve new technology, or new thoughts – which had been a real problem at art school – so I could bluff my way through. My marks dropped off but I was still doing well enough. The real problem now wasn't studying. It was the thoughts of self-harm.

At first I thought I could control the fantasies but they were beginning to take over. Sometimes I gave into them, and was then safe while the wound healed. But I was physically healthy, so this usually didn't take long. The images, when they came back, became worse the longer I resisted them. I didn't just think of carving up my arms anymore. I began to picture cutting off fingers and standing at the mirror, slashing my face. It was at this point that I rang the helpline – and discovered that my thoughts weren't something I could talk about, even to an anonymous stranger at the other end of the phone.

My doctor made a booking for me with the visiting specialist who did mental health assessments once a month at the university health centre. My first visit to a psychiatrist was not a success. I arrived late, antagonistic and hung-over; so hung-over that I had to dash out of the surgery to throw up.

The psychiatrist looked at my file, looked at me, and asked a few questions about my drinking habits and drug use. 'Is there anything else you want to tell me?'

I didn't like her. She was cold, dismissive and I had no desire to tell her anything. 'No.'

'My advice then is to cut down on the drinking. I don't think you need therapy. I'd suggest you keep taking the antidepressants and talk to your doctor if necessary.'

And with that, the consultation was over.

During my next visit to my doctor, I admitted that I hadn't presented my case very well. I hadn't told the psychiatrist anything very much: certainly not what was worrying me. She gave me another referral. It was someone she didn't know personally, but she said to let her know if there were any problems.

Two weeks later, I caught the train out to Bondi Junction. His office was on the tenth floor, looking back towards the city. It could have been that of an accountant. The furniture looked as though it had been picked up at a government auction and there were few books. I immediately felt uneasy.

First of all he asked me questions about my age, education, family and general health. He then asked me to describe my symptoms.

'Right,' he said. 'I'd like you to do a few tests to determine what your short-term memory is like and how your general cognitive abilities are.'

After that, I told him about my desire to hurt myself – including the more recent graphic images – and he handed me a pamphlet. 'Read this carefully, and we can talk about it when you see me next week. I don't believe it's depression you're suffering from. It might be a form of schizophrenia though. You can make an appointment with my receptionist.' He stood up, which was apparently my signal to leave.

I was shaking on the way home as I read the pamphlet, appalled and terrified. All I knew about schizophrenia was that it was associated with homelessness, and that people who suffered from it were put in mental hospitals. Was this going to happen to me? Were these thoughts going to become worse? Was this why I couldn't control them anymore?

I couldn't believe it.

I told Alex that night. He didn't believe it either. 'The man's a fucking dickhead. Don't go back to him. You're not schizophrenic – but you're certainly not well. Find someone who can treat you properly.'

Chapter Three

I was desperate. I started off miserable but was now scared as well. It was clear that I needed to find a decent specialist.

I'd recently seen my old family doctor while visiting my parents, and had mentioned that I was taking antidepressants. He'd immediately scribbled the contact details of a colleague on a piece of paper, saying she was great, and if I felt I needed any more help, she was the person to contact.

After scrabbling around in the shoebox of receipts, letters and bank statements on my desk, I found her number. I don't know how long I sat on the stairs staring at it, too nervous to call. I wasn't frightened of her but of the fact that maybe she couldn't help me. An increasingly large part of me believed that this was it, this was my life and it wasn't going to get better. The problem was me.

I didn't want that part of me to be proved right, so forced myself to make the call to my third psychiatrist in two months.

It was around 6.30 pm, and she was still at work. I introduced myself, and explained what the problem was. Initially, I was embarrassed but gradually, as she asked about how I felt, about what I had done, and about my family, I felt more comfortable. She was listening and taking me seriously.

And then she threw me into a complete spin, saying, 'It sounds like it would be beneficial for you to have a brief stint in hospital.' My doctor had mentioned this possibility before but I'd dismissed the idea. I didn't want to. I didn't need to. I was not sick.

The psychiatrist phrased it as though it would just be a break, some 'time out'. She also thought I needed to be properly assessed and it was obvious I wasn't coping. 'Can you hold on for an hour or so while I make a few calls?' she asked.

I said yes, but wasn't convinced she'd ring back.

She did. At 7.30 pm she called to confirm that a bed would be available the following day at N_, a private psychiatric clinic. The word 'clinic' rather than hospital didn't make it any more appealing.

I scribbled down the address and listened as she gave me directions for the next morning. In the meantime, I was told not to make any decisions bigger than what to wear or what to eat for dinner. Most importantly, I wasn't to harm myself.

She suggested that I ask a friend to keep me company for the evening, and then go to bed early. I just needed to get through the next twelve hours.

I promised her I'd look after myself, then put down the phone, relieved but shaking. What little knowledge I had of mental hospitals came from films like *One Flew Over the Cuckoo's Nest* and *Frances*. I had visions of people shuffling around in their pyjamas, drugged into tranquillity. I thought of bars on windows, linoleum floors and the invasive smell of disinfectant. But if that was what it took to stop me hurting myself, then I was prepared to submit.

I didn't call anyone. I had never intended to. It was too hard to deal with other people, particularly those I knew. On the one hand I didn't want to spread my miserable feelings; on the other, I couldn't disguise them anymore. I felt like a leper and it was better just to stay out of the way. I did go to bed early though, my mind whirling as I stared at the buttercup walls. In a moment of enthusiasm when I'd first moved in, I'd painted them. It felt like they were ridiculing me in their cheerfulness. But finally something was going to happen. It was all about to be taken out of my hands.

I fell asleep exhausted.

Rodney was home when I woke up the next morning. I was going to have to say something about going away. I could kill two birds with one stone: he had a car so I could get a lift and I could also tell him a bit about what was going on in my head, not the thoughts of self-harm of course, but the depression. I could stop pretending that things were okay. Pretending was not only exhausting, it was also making me dislike Rodney intensely. Somehow I felt that it was his fault I couldn't be honest. No-one talks about self-harm, so no-one talks about self-harm. It's still a taboo subject – and no wonder. I certainly didn't want to burden anyone with what was happening in my head. It was too graphic, too frightening. It wasn't fair to talk about it.

While he understood the idea of depression, Rodney seemed surprised that I should need to go to hospital. I looked fine. Nevertheless, he was happy to drive me there. He wasn't happy to come in: we weren't friends after all, just flatmates. Rodney left me and my small suitcase on the footpath outside a large grey building with dark tinted windows. If not for the sign saying 'Ambulances this way' it could have been an office block.

Initially, I couldn't even find the reception area. The café on the ground floor was closed and there seemed to be nowhere else to ask for directions. The place was deserted and all I wanted to do was sit down and cry. It wasn't fair; this was too hard. Going to hospital was supposed to make me feel better, not worse. I was there though. I'd made the effort and I wasn't going to let a small thing like not being able to find the entrance put me off. Besides, I wasn't up to going home. And then I saw the lift. It had been in front of me the entire time, along with a few chairs, pot plants, several unmarked doors and a sign listing the floors and wards. I got in and pressed the button for Level 3, reception, my hand shaking. It wasn't too late to change my mind.

But I didn't.

Level 3 was carpeted and painted in what the decorators must have thought were soothing shades of apricot. I went through two heavy doors, both of which had glass panels at face height. (I learnt later that these doors could be locked electronically from reception.) At the end of the corridor I could see several nurses in uniform and various other people milling about. I headed in that direction. Like a movie in slow motion, it seemed to take forever to reach them. I felt sick, weak and pathetic. What kept going over and over in my mind was that I was physically well and that this was a hospital. I had no need to be there.

The clinic normally didn't admit people on the weekends, which was why the downstairs reception was closed. I was expected though. I bit the inside of my cheek and followed a friendly nurse to a room with four beds, each with its own chest of drawers, bedside table and curtain that could be pulled around for privacy. I was to discover that while the curtain hid you, it didn't offer any protection from the people who talked constantly, in their sleep as well as in their waking hours. Nor did it protect you from those who were simply curious.

I was asked the usual health questions. Had I had any major operations? Was I allergic to anything? Had I had any infectious diseases? They asked for my medication. I was also asked if I'd brought in any sharp implements. Why would I do that? I thought, I'm trying to get away from those things. They know that. A psychiatrist who would assess me more fully would be coming in later. In the meantime, I was told to stay on the ward, either in my corner of the room – a space of about one and a half by two metres – or in the common area.

Contrary to what I had imaged, the common area wasn't filled with people dribbling and muttering to themselves. Instead, five or six women sat on plastic-covered chairs and sofas. They watched television in a rather half-hearted way, read old copies of women's magazines and *Reader's Digests*, and talked quietly in a manner that suggested they didn't want to disturb any-one else. Most of the women in this peach-coloured room with its matching floral curtains were in their sixties. It was strange to see them, dressed and looking perfectly well, sitting patiently inside on a cloudless, sunny morning.

This wasn't what I had expected. My immediate reaction was, I'm going to be really bored. It hadn't occurred to me to think about how I'd fill my time once I signed in.

I was also trapped. I was now, of my own volition, locked up. I was not to leave the ward, let alone the floor or the building. I wasn't allowed to duck down to the shops. I couldn't go for a walk. This was particu-larly galling as exercise was probably my only 'appro-priate' way of coping with stress. I'd never quite been able to get rid of the idea – which first surfaced when I stopped eating as a teenager – that if you didn't exer-cise every day you'd get fat. Just like that. Sometimes I could ignore it but the more unhappy I was, the more it recurred.

It was strange being in a hospital where you could get out of bed – indeed where you were expected to do so – but where you had nowhere to go and nothing to do. On Monday, I was to find that there was plenty to do. There were groups to attend on anger manage-ment, medications, coping with depression, dealing with anxiety. But on the weekend most people, if they could, would get overnight leave and spend the time with their families, or at least arrange to go out for a meal. For those who stayed behind, the two days dragged on endlessly.

What had I done? I still didn't believe I was sick. I was perfectly healthy, just unhappy. What was I doing in this place full of sad, lonely old women? How had this happened?

Late in the day, the consulting psychiatrist turned up. The doctor who had arranged for me to be admitted wasn't taking on new patients, nor was she a visiting specialist at this hospital. I couldn't imagine how she'd got me in. Now this slight, well-dressed man in his fifties, Dr G, was going to take over my treatment.

Dr G asked me to tell him about myself. As usual, I left out the bits I didn't consider anyone else's business, such as my love life and my mistrust of the medical profession. I was too embarrassed to talk about sex or relationships, and only touched on drug use. I circled around issues and expected him to read my mind, pick up on clues. He scribbled down notes but didn't make any comments.

At the end of our session, he asked me to sign a contract: a list of ten points, things that I would agree not to do during my 'stay'. These points included not harming myself, either with a blade or in any other way. I wasn't to harm anyone else, nor was I to leave the ward without permission. There were other requirements but they seemed unimportant. It was a boilerplate contract, designed to cover a range of patients. Dr G highlighted the clauses relevant to me. Were I to break the terms of this contract it would give him, as my specialist, the authority to ask me to leave or, chillingly, to have me 'scheduled'. To be scheduled is to be placed, involuntarily, in a state mental hospital (in some states this is called 'being sectioned'). Once there, only your doctor or a mental health review board can decide when you leave. The doors are locked, the windows are barred and the patients can be violent and psychotic. Understaffing and underfunding mean that these places can be more akin to jails than hospitals.

Like an obedient child, I signed on the dotted line and promised to behave myself. This was the beginning of a period of learned helplessness. Suddenly, after a long struggle to maintain the appearance of coping, I didn't have to look after myself. Someone would remind me to take my medication. I would be given afternoon tea, morning tea and supper, as well as cooked meals. Dinner was at 5.40 pm in the dining room, so supper at 8 pm was a necessity. Breakfast was between 7.30 and 8 am. The only people allowed meals in bed were those too unwell to get up. I wasn't considered one of them.

Over the next few weeks my days were filled with group therapy, which I grew to hate. I really wasn't interested in the other patients. I wanted my problem solved; I didn't care about theirs. I began to behave like a fourteen-year-old, alternately giggling and sullen. The environment seemed to encourage this behaviour.

I discovered that three of us in the Acute Ward had problems with self-mutilation and were there for observation and our own protection. What we had in common was gender, age and no confirmed psychiatric diagnosis. Annabel, Jessica and I were simply unhappy. Self-harm, or specifically self-mutilation, isn't classified as a disorder in itself. It is seen as part of something else, such as a depressive disorder, an eating disorder, or some kind of personality disorder.

The women I'd seen on that first Saturday weren't really representative of those on the ward. They were just the ones who didn't have anywhere to go. In Acute – where I'd been placed – people suffered from a range of conditions, most with frightening names and very specific treatment regimes. Some patients had severe clinical depression, others were changing medication, and there were also those who were waiting for medication to kick in. There were those with bipolar disorder who were in the manic phase and had to be sedated to curb their behaviour which could be extremely damaging. Some believed they could fly, or were extremely promiscuous. Others had delusions of enormous power. Given this mix of patients, the ward was surprisingly quiet. I don't think this was just a result of the sound-absorbent carpet.

The girls and women who suffered from eating disorders were on the floor upstairs. There were no men up there. I watched them walk into the dining room, accompanied by nurses who made sure they didn't hide the food in their pockets or under the plates. After meals they were made to lie down to let the food digest. Those who had been there for some time looked healthy – not exactly plump, but no longer thin. Others, newly arrived, did not look like young women. Their hair was lank, their features gaunt and their posture stooped. One girl could no longer walk and instead sat motionlessly in a wheelchair. Looking at them, I knew I'd had a close call.

But then I'd chosen another fork in the road to self-destruction.

There were only two places you could meet people from the other wards: the dining room and the recreation room downstairs. While people didn't tend to socialise when eating, they did chat as they played pool or smoked. Smoking was the norm; if people didn't when they came in, there was a fair chance they would when they went out. In the recreation room, those from Acute could beg cigarettes from Eating Disorders who could be sure to get them from the Alcohol and Drug Addictions crowd.

It was down there too, out of the way of the hospital staff, that you'd hear other people's stories. Some were horrific and some, like mine, were disturbingly mundane. There was a hierarchy of disorders, and I'd regularly hear:

'You're not really in danger, it's not like cutting your arm will kill you, is it? None of those scars are real suicide attempts are they? You're just playing. If you wanted to kill yourself you'd try some other way.'

We self-mutilators had no real tag but quickly began to want one. We wanted a name for our problem, a clear-cut category and label. That would give us an explanation and, no doubt, a quick drug-based cure. We didn't want to hear that we had borderline personality disorder, or any other personality disorders. These were too intangible and, worse, there would be no quick solution with that diagnosis. But it wasn't straightforward, and my treatment program highlighted this.

My new psychiatrist, Dr G, believed my urge to self-harm was exacerbated by depression, so he 'put' me on Prozac, as the Prothiaden clearly hadn't worked. An antidepressant was necessary if I wanted to feel better, I was told. He also prescribed Stelazine, which I was to take to calm me down if I felt that I needed to harm myself.

Psychotherapy wasn't, at that point, seen as a way to solve my problems. The argument went that even if I delved back into my past and found something monstrous, knowing about it, and discussing it, wasn't necessarily going to stop the urge to self-harm. Dr G, having decided that there wasn't anything obvious causing my problem, decided to focus on the immediate issue: how to stop me cutting myself. The key seemed to be in breaking the pattern. I had told him how it worked.

For days or weeks, I would resist the urge to hurt myself, and then, for some reason, I would be unable to do so any longer. I'd walk to the nearest chemist and buy a new packet of razor blades. I'd use one and then throw the rest out, horrified by what I'd done. While the wound healed I'd feel better. And then the cycle would start all over again. Dr G's suggestions included calling someone before I went to the chemist, or walking to the nearest café instead of buying blades.

It was apparent that he really had no idea how best to treat me.

At the end of the first week, my risk assessment was changed, and I was allowed to go for walks. Administratively, this meant that I graduated from a blue to a red dot on the large whiteboard that was fixed to the wall opposite the nurses' station. This board listed the first name of every patient in Acute, their room number and their bed number. The coloured sticker indicated how sick (or dangerous) the patient was. Blue meant that you were confined to the ward, orange that you could leave if escorted by a nurse or family member, and red was for those who were allowed out for limited periods of time unaccompanied. It was, in theory, a sensible system but in practice it had its problems – it was easy to switch the stickers around when the nurses weren't looking.

With the notable exception of those who were manic, most of the other patients were polite and quiet – an effect, I guess, of both their illness and their medication. Occasionally there were disturbances. One male patient liked to sit in his tracksuit in the common room masturbating while watching television. Many of us had reported this, but it wasn't until he attacked a nurse that he was moved, we assumed, to a more secure location. Jessica, who had signed a contract like mine, broke it when she managed to create two sets of raw red scratch marks on the inner side of both arms, using her fingernails which she'd carefully filed. Within ten minutes of these marks being noticed, she was assessed and scheduled. She was distraught.

First the police turned up, motorbike helmets under their arms, followed by ambulance officers carrying a stretcher. Technically, Jessica was now under government 'protection' and proper procedures had to be followed. This meant that she had to have a police escort. But Jessica wasn't mad or dangerous. She was just miserable and expressing it. It seemed to us that her behaviour had been seen by hospital authorities as attention-seeking and she was being punished for it. I heard later that she was spending her days curled up in the corner of a large common room like a scared animal. It was a warning for those of us who had signed the same agreements.

It didn't take more than a few days for the outside world to recede. I didn't watch the news or listen to the radio or read any newspapers. I didn't read at all, in fact. I couldn't concentrate enough to do so. I gave up after the fourth attempt at the first chapter of a Jackie Collins novel. I felt as though I were in a bubble. We could have been on Mars for all that normal life mattered.

There were few visitors. Rodney didn't call, Alex didn't call. Only Peter, one of the few people I was still in touch with from uni, dropped in. When I rang him to let him know where I was he wasn't really surprised. Instead, he sounded relieved. He knew that things had been difficult for me, and had been doing his best to help. I didn't tell him much about what was going on in my head but he guessed a lot of it, and was as supportive as I'd let him be. This meant that sometimes I would ring him at ten at night, frightened I'd use the fresh blade sitting on my desk. He'd always come over when I called. Often I didn't ring him though. I couldn't, or didn't want to.

Peter thought hospital sounded like an excellent place for me.

I still remember him walking into the common room; it must have been on a Saturday afternoon because he was wearing tennis gear. He sat down on the plastic-coated couch and started chatting to the person next to him, gradually including others in the conversation. Everyone was charmed of course, and I was really pleased. It was the first sign of normality I'd seen for a while. He was behaving as if he'd been invited to afternoon tea at an aunt's house. He was being considerate – which was more than I could say for my parents.

My mother visited me once while I was in hospital. While she brought flowers and a pair of new pyjamas as a peace offering, we had little to say to each other. My admission to hospital was just another example of how weak I was. Hadn't they taught me how to 'rise above it'? Hadn't they shown me how to hide and ignore my problems? My mother believed that I was choosing to be like this. Choosing not to cheer up, not to make an effort, and, finally, choosing to hurt myself.

When I arrived in hospital, I agreed with her view. By the time I left a month later, I didn't. There had to be a reason this was happening to me and I wanted to know what it was.

Chapter Four

I arrived home with antidepressants, what I assumed were tranquillisers, and another script that I'd put in my bag without even bothering to read. Hospital hadn't cured me but it had given me a rest. As I walked in through the kitchen and up the stairs it dawned on me that despite the paint job, the flat was dark, dank and smelt of too many burned vegetarian curries. Rodney wasn't home.

My room was stuffy and I could hear the noise of the traffic as it roared past on the road out the front. Looking around I noticed that I hadn't painted the walls very well. There were sections in the corners and near the ceiling where the underlying beige showed through. I also hadn't bothered to tidy up before I left. A half-empty vodka bottle stood beside my futon with its hopelessly cheery red and white checked doona I'd made in preparation for my new life in Sydney.

I remember being so excited about the move, and, when I'd first arrived, I had loved it all. I had been happy. My first year at university was a constant round of parties, pubs and gossip. Lectures rarely featured.

For the first time in years I ate cake, ice-cream, choco-late and, well, anything else that was on offer. I slept until ten, often taking an afternoon nap as well. It was wonderful – but did have its downside.

By second year, I'd already put on weight so I decided that there was no harm in drinking. Besides, I'd probably throw up at the end of the evening any-way and if I didn't there was always the 'no calorie' theory to fall back on. Discovering alcohol changed my social life entirely. I discovered what countless oth-ers before me had: that it makes you feel great. Until it doesn't. Drinking also made me much less shy around men, and I regularly found myself struggling to remember exactly who it was that I'd had a fling with the previous evening. Flings didn't ever develop into anything else however, and the reason didn't always involve poor judgment on my part.

Sober, I didn't trust men at all and they were par-tially to blame for this.

Bands of guys would walk, or drive, around the campus taunting girls like me, girls who weren't their ideal. I had glasses, I wasn't thin – but didn't have big boobs to compensate – and I was shy. Sometimes it would be three in the afternoon and I'd be walking back from a lecture when I'd hear them. They didn't ever touch me, or even come too close. They didn't even yell suggestions such as 'show us your tits' or 'suck my cock'. Their obscenities were more basic, less imaginative than this. They just yelled out nouns: 'cunt', 'bushpig' or 'fat moll'.

Unlike some of my friends, I didn't grow to hate them as, secretly, I agreed with what they said. I believed I was fat and unattractive. And the weekly calls from my mother didn't help as there were three questions that she never failed to ask, no matter what else was discussed. Have you lost weight? Have you had any results? Have you got a boyfriend?

The answer to each question was always no.

Despite this, I did enjoy myself. And passed.

Things were very different now. The antidepressants still didn't seem to help, but I forced myself to keep going. I attended seminars, ate a bit, enough to keep going but no more as food just didn't interest me. And drank a bit. I visited Dr G once a week and started seeing Alex again. Things were still difficult but at least I had stopped caring about my relationship with him, such as it was. I had other things on my mind. Self-harm, and thinking about it, became a form of escape.

It took about three weeks before I injured myself again. In one way it was something that no longer scared me; in another it was terrifying. I didn't know what my limits were. Some days, it was enough just to know that I had a packet of blades in the house. They were a cold, very sharp, security blanket. Other days, instead of using them I'd call Peter, who I still relied on, to get rid of them. This interrupted the pattern as Dr G advised, but it didn't take away the desire. And sometimes, the desire was just too much.

Felix had been at art school with me, a couple of years ahead. To get himself through financially, he stacked shelves in a supermarket several nights a week. To get through that – and to stay awake in class – he used speed. A lot of it. He was busy, jumpy and with only three months to go before finishing his degree, very stressed. So he asked me to write an essay for him. Or to be more accurate, Alex asked me to write an essay for him: they lived together.

Obviously I should have said no. It wasn't only against the rules; I didn't know the subject. I was also having trouble just doing my own work, and holding my life together. There were two reasons I said yes: one was the money and the other was Alex. He believed I'd do a good job and I was flattered. So I agreed to write 3000 words about a controversial contemporary Australian artist and Felix agreed to pick it up two weeks later.

Within hours, I was having not just doubts but stomach cramps.

The following Saturday I visited a small gallery where the artist was holding an exhibition. The work was crude and shocking. I sighed, and left to find a café where I could re-read the lecture notes Felix had given me. At least his handwriting was legible. I scribbled a few ideas in the margins and then started to read a magazine.

Over the next few days I felt more and more compelled to harm myself but knowing a cut would affect my ability to type, I held off. My own deadline of a week went by and I realised that I wasn't just holding back from hurting myself but from writing as well. Then there was just one day to go. I had no choice. I had made an agreement and I had a responsibility to carry it out, no matter how I felt. So I started writing. Writing anything that came into my head, conscious all the time that this was someone else's final-year essay in a course I'd never taken. What if I couldn't do it? What if it didn't make sense? What if it failed?

Shit. Shit. Shit. I had never had an essay fail in my life before but I had also never been in this position. I had always been either prepared or at least confident enough to bluff my way through. But if it failed, what would Alex think? He obviously believed I was smart and this was something to hang on to, something that didn't fluctuate like weight, and wasn't subjective like looks. If this essay was failed, it would prove I was stupid, would ruin Felix's grades, and would affect Alex's relationship with him – and with me. All of these thoughts ran through my head as I tried to write, feeling sicker and sicker as I went on. The deception also worried me. I still thought of myself as a good, ethical person. I got cranky when I saw someone throw rubbish on the ground rather than put it in the bin.

I sat at the desk in the corner of my room, vodka beside the computer, typing desperately through the night and into the following morning. By 4 pm the next day it was done. I couldn't re-read it, not even to check for typos. So I printed it out – carefully not looking at the text – and put the pages, with a disk, in a folder so at least it looked neat.

Then I decided that it was time to get out the razor. Cutting was the only thing that would make me feel better; there was no other way I could handle being with myself anymore. I was disgusted that I had agreed to write the essay in the first place and embarrassed that I didn't even know whether it was any good. I hated – hated – the fact that it wasn't my responsibility.

Felix was due to turn up at 5 pm but that didn't matter: a part of me even wanted him to see what his request had forced me to do.

I got out some old newspapers and put them on the kitchen table, then went upstairs to get a new packet of blades. I opened it and got one out. As I unwrapped the waxed paper I felt simultaneously elated and ill. It was too late to stop. Maybe this could have been averted. Perhaps if the shop assistant hadn't said, as I'd bought the packet, 'Things that bad, eh?' And then laughed.

Different people have different ways of hurting themselves, and even those who cut themselves don't all do it in the same way. There are many different techniques. I only used razor blades now. They were clean, sharp and disposable. Annabel, from the hospital, only used surgical scalpels – and others I know used knives. Princess Diana was reported to have used not only a pocketknife but in one tragic moment, a vegetable peeler.

I pushed the blade across my wrist, more deeply than ever before, conscious that it had to be worse than the last cut. Every cut had to be worse than the one before. I've heard of people who would create exactly the same mark every time, so that they'd have a line of identical scars, and others who would constantly attack the same scar, opening up the wound again and again. This wasn't the way I did it – perhaps because I needed to see a progression. In that sense, this one was a success: it was nasty. I knew that immediately.

At first I just sat and stared at the bloody, gaping line, relieved and envigorated. I'd done it, and it was over. Next I found a tea towel, wrapped my wrist up tightly and put the newspapers in the bin. Feeling light-headed, I got a beer out of the fridge and wandered up to the balcony where I waited. All of the pent-up stress of the last two weeks had melted away: my throbbing wrist took my full attention.

A few minutes later I heard the jangling sound of the fork mobile that we used as a doorbell. I went to my room, picked up the folder, and, somewhat gingerly, walked downstairs. It was Felix.

We had a bit of a chat and I asked if he'd like a beer. 'Excellent idea,' was his response. As we sat looking at the city skyline I told him about the essay. I was able to be coherent and specific. I warned him to proofread it thoroughly. 'Of course,' he said, evidently very pleased that it existed at all. It hadn't occurred to me until then that he'd had his own doubts about whether I'd do it.

After about twenty minutes, during which I talked incessantly, I motioned towards the tea towel. I could barely move my arm now and blood was beginning to seep through. 'I have a little problem.'

To my surprise, he agreed: I'd thought that he hadn't noticed. 'Is it bad?' He was very calm.

I considered this question for a moment. 'I'm not sure. Yes. It's not life-threatening but it'll need stitches.' And then I realised the real reason I'd done it before he arrived. 'Would you mind coming to the medical centre with me? It's not really fair to ask, but I want to make sure they don't try and lock me up. If I have someone with me I should be okay.'

'Sure. Happy to.' He paused. 'Are they that tough?'

'Different doctors react in different ways. It just depends. I've been lucky so far, but there's been some close calls.'

He then told me that Alex had mentioned 'my problem'. It explained why he was so calm. Secretly, I was furious. It just wasn't Alex's business to talk about this. He had no right.

The medical centre was full of people coughing and sniffling. We sat as far away from them as possible and entertained ourselves by doing a Cleo relationship quiz. Things didn't look good for me and Alex.

When, finally, it was my turn to see the doctor, I sat down and calmly unwrapped my wrist. 'It could be worse but I think it probably needs stitches.' It could have been someone else's arm I was talking about.

He looked at it and agreed. He also glanced at the pinky-red scars surrounding it, and asked how it had happened.

I was direct: 'I cut myself.'

He didn't say much for a bit, instead he got on to cleaning it, injecting the local anaesthetic – which really stung – and stitching it up.

I chatted constantly and even, I remember, told him jokes.

After he'd bandaged it he sat down at his desk and looked at me. 'Are you sure someone else didn't do this?'

I told him no, that I'd done it myself, and that I wouldn't do it again. He didn't look as though he believed me and instead asked if I was seeing a special-ist. I gave him Dr G's name. 'I'll have to notify him, you know.' He then asked if I had someone to look after me. I told him that Felix was in the waiting room, adding for good measure, 'I'll be fine'. I would be for a while anyway. I just didn't know for how long.

By the time we left the surgery it was getting dark and Felix suggested that we have dinner. I was in high spirits, due no doubt to the various natural painkillers that were flowing around my body in response to my attack on it. Felix was also relaxed and, crisis over, we sat down to a delicious meal. When he walked me home later, Felix said, obviously surprised, that he'd had a great time. So had I.

And therein lay the problem and the cause of what was quite obviously now an addiction: harming myself really did make me feel better. Not permanently, but for a short time. After I'd hurt myself it could be weeks before I did it again. That initial pain, and the following period of constantly feeling and seeing the wound before me, kept everything else at bay. It was as if I could channel everything negative into that bandage. All I had to do was look at it and I felt better.

Chapter Five

I was fine for a couple of weeks. Fine in the sense that I didn't injure myself, not that I was well. Or well-adjusted. In fact, I was finding it more and more difficult to do even ordinary things like grocery shopping and laundry. My relationship with Alex was still structured around alcohol and sporadic 3 am visits, followed by daylight rejection. Even through my haze I could see it was pretty awful, and certainly not helping.

What I really wanted was some peace: a respite from everything.

Then one afternoon I remembered that I had some Stelazine in the house, and I recalled being told to take it if I felt like hurting myself. Normally the desire to hurt myself overrode the desire to take something that might stop it, so I'd not used the medication before. I'd thrown the bottle, like so many other things, onto my desk. There weren't very many pills in it and I didn't take them all, just a few. Not even a handful. I didn't want to accidentally overdose.

Just after I'd swallowed them Alex called. I told him I'd taken something to knock me out. 'Not too much I hope?' he said, half-serious.

'No, not too much.'

When I put down the phone it was about five in the afternoon. I went to bed.

My alarm went off the next morning and I forced myself to get up, feeling like I did most Sunday mornings: hung-over. As I sat on the bus on the way to my part-time job at the gallery, I ate my toast and stared out of the window, registering nothing.

There was a big surrealist exhibition on so it was bound to be busy. There'd be queues of people. 'At least', I said to one of the girls I worked with in the shop, 'the time'll go faster'.

Just after we'd opened the doors, my eyes started rolling upwards. I'd roll them down, and immediately, they'd go up again. It was as though they were drawn to a magnet somewhere above my head. I had no idea what was happening, and no memory of the previous evening.

Thinking something to drink might help, I took my mid-morning break early and walked quietly over to the temporary exhibition café where I bought a cup of tea. After several attempts, it became obvious that I couldn't drink it, not without spilling it. There was nothing to do but go back to the shop. I didn't feel faint, I didn't feel sick and I was being paid by the hour, so I kept working.

After another thirty minutes of serving people who politely ignored my problem, I realised that it was getting worse. My neck began to tilt back, just like my eyes. The only way to hold it down was with my hands, which made working the cash register very difficult. Perhaps, I thought, if I go on my lunch break and have some food, it will stop.

My colleagues didn't argue and I was soon outside in the park, in the fresh air. After buying my regular lunch – a small carrot muffin and a bottle of water – I found a secluded place and sat down to eat. Strangely, although I had no idea what was happening to me, I was quite calm. I was embarrassed though, particularly when a group of schoolboys plonked themselves down less than two metres away. They furtively lit up. It just wasn't fair. All I wanted was a little privacy and thinking space. Sighing, I picked up my bag and went back inside. The truth was I knew that something wasn't quite right. I couldn't eat, I couldn't drink and I couldn't control my neck and eye muscles. It was time to try lying down.

I asked at the information desk about a sick room. The woman told me to wait for a guard downstairs, that the door was next to the women's loos. After letting the girls in the shop know where I was, I stood, holding my head still, waiting for the guard with the key. People streamed past, going to the bathrooms, to the exhibition and to the shop. They tried not to look at me. Eventually, the guard arrived and opened the door into a small white room with a bed against one wall and a few boxes against another. There were no windows.

Lying down seemed to help and for a while I felt a little better. One of my colleagues brought in a glass of water and asked if I was okay. Not exactly, I told her, then thanked her for asking. I just needed a bit more time. I'd be out soon.

And then, just as I thought I was going to fall asleep, the muscles in my back began to spasm. My back started arching. It was as though I was having some kind of slow motion fit. This obviously wasn't a good sign.

Another of the girls came in. She frowned. 'You really don't look well, Vic. Would a Panadol help?'

I shook my head and she left.

The problem was that I didn't know what would help. If I could just work out what was happening, then maybe I'd know what to do. As I was thinking, my boss came in. She usually didn't work weekends, and given that she could be very scary, we liked it that way. What was she doing here now?

'What have you taken?' she asked.

Bloody hell, I thought, what did she think of me? Did I look like a drug addict? I thought I hid things pretty well.

'Nothing. I haven't taken anything.' I said.

She didn't believe me. 'Well, whatever the problem is, you need to see a doctor. I'll call you a taxi.' And then she paused. 'Can you actually walk?'

I now realised that I wasn't even going to be able to stand up. Walking would be impossible. It was also becoming more difficult to speak. 'No. No.'

'Then I'm going to call you an ambulance.' She walked out, quietly shutting the door behind her.

Within minutes a paramedic arrived. The first thing he asked was what I'd taken. I didn't understand, why was everyone so convinced I'd taken something? 'Nothing' was all I could say. As the paramedic was taking my pulse, two ambulance officers came in. The room was getting crowded.

'What's she taken?' one of them asked.

'Don't know, she won't say. Looks like a dystonic reaction.'

As the ambos helped me onto the stretcher, one of them suggested they put a sheet over my head. We were going to have to walk through the exhibition crowds to get out, and it might save me a bit of embarrassment. I must have looked stunned, as he quickly added, 'Just joking'. It was humiliating, but I did feel better. At least I was being looked after. And they seemed to know what was wrong.

As I lay in the back of the ambulance trying not to convulse, the officers chatted to me, relentlessly cheerful. 'Life can't be that bad luv.' Had I really overdosed? I was confused. It wasn't as though you'd forget something like that, was it?

Suddenly I remembered something. 'I took a Prozac this morning.'

'Do you take them regularly?' one of the officers asked.

'Yep.'

On reaching the hospital I was transferred to a bed in the emergency ward. The place was quiet. A young doctor came over to me and asked what I'd taken. I was getting sick of this question.

This time I made a huge effort. 'Beyond a Prozac this morning, nothing. I don't remember taking anything.'

He confirmed what the paramedic had said: I was having a dystonic reaction. He then said there was an antidote available and was sure it would work. He left for a minute and then came back with a syringe. 'This should calm things down,' he said. He then pulled the curtains and I was left alone.

A little while later a nurse looked in. 'Feeling any better?'

My back arched again.

'Right, well, don't worry, it should start to work soon.'

Later still, I began to think that maybe this was it. Maybe my muscles would be in permanent spasm. Perhaps this was the onset of some kind of disease. Or perhaps I had taken something, as they were all suggesting, and had brought it on myself. Maybe it was like when I was a child and made a face. My mother used to say the wind might change and then I'd be stuck looking like that. Was this to be it?

As I lay there, my mind lurching from one awful possibility to another, the doctor returned. He smiled, before telling me that he was going to give me another injection. I wasn't responding in quite the way he'd hoped. I knew he really meant 'You're not responding at all'.

Ten or so minutes later, the doctor appeared again. Still my head was tilting backwards by itself. He looked more serious this time, as though he were making a decision. 'Let's give things a little bit longer, shall we?' It was a rhetorical question. I wasn't in any position to argue.

As I lay there, I desperately tried to remember the evening before but nothing came to me. Nothing at all. And then I realised that the tension had gone. I tentatively moved my head from side to side. It did as I wanted. My eyes and back seemed fine. It was over.

The doctor clearly looked relieved. 'Ah, you're looking better at last. How are you feeling?'

I smiled weakly, 'Okay, thanks. Just tired.'

He then asked for the name of my doctor, and, if I had one, my psychiatrist. He wanted to notify both of them. I gave him their names, for once not worried about being scheduled, as I was still convinced that this wasn't my fault.

'I'll get the nurse to change the dressing on your wrist as well. Although you should be okay now, I'd suggest that you stay here for a while until you feel stronger.' He turned to leave, and then stopped. 'Of course if the symptoms return, come back immediately.'

Come back? I lay on the cot in the emergency ward for a couple of hours worrying about the doctor's parting comment. I didn't know what had brought this on so how did I know that it wouldn't happen again? When I was sure that I felt okay, I left and caught a bus home. As I sat next to the window, trying not to cry, I remembered the Stelazine. I also remembered the other prescription I had been given with it, but had never bothered to have filled. They'd given it to me in case the drug gave me any side effects.

I found out much later that Stelazine wasn't an ordinary tranquilliser but an antipsychotic. Later still I was told that this medication wasn't just prescribed for hallucinations, but to control aggression.

Chapter Six

During the worst periods, when my mind seemed to be seething with destructive images, I avoided people. It was too difficult to pretend I was coping, and I was determined not to burden anyone I cared about with my problems. Besides, most people I knew were wary of me now – they thought I was mad, sick or dangerous. Just because I didn't talk about things, it didn't mean other people didn't hear of them. Alex and Peter, and sometimes an old family friend, Catherine, were the exceptions. All were practical, pragmatic and difficult to shock. I could rely on them not to make me feel guilty about what I was doing – or at least no more guilty than I already felt.

The one person I was supposed to be able to confide in fully was my psychiatrist, Dr G.

Every week I would catch the train across the bridge and walk down to his rooms from the station. I'd sit, hiding behind a pot plant pretending to read old copies of *National Geographic* in order not to have to look at the other people waiting. When he opened the door and asked me to come in, I always stood up with a slight feeling of excitement. Every week I went in with the expectation that at the end of the 50-minute session I would be cured without ever having to do anything, that magically, I would walk out content, confident and happy, with no interest in harming myself.

There was a complication that made this unlikely: I treated him as an opponent, not a resource, and I didn't trust him. There were two reasons for this. He maintained that antidepressants were the only way to fix me – and they evidently weren't helping – and I found him patronising. This meant I behaved uncharacteristically childishly and wasn't honest in my weekly therapy sessions. I told him about my urges to hurt myself, but not about Alex. He advised me to keep up with friends and go out, to keep doing normal things, no matter how hard it felt. I told him I was doing this. Lying was easier than arguing.

Then one day, I visited Dr G in an unusually cheerful mood.

After what seemed like an eternity sitting in his waiting room, he asked me into his office. I looked around. I fidgeted in my chair, staring at my purple stockings and tiny blue suede miniskirt, watching my left foot with the green shoe swinging. I smiled at him. 'What's up?'

He raised an eyebrow warily. 'You seem cheerful. What have you been doing?'

'I don't know. This and that. Shopping, going out, drinking, seeing people. The usual stuff.' I shrugged and noticed for the first time the view outside his window. It was of a graveyard.

'Not for you, Vic. Not since I've known you. Can you tell me a little more about how you feel?' He seemed almost suspicious.

'How I feel? How I feel. How do I feel? It's a good question.' The words tumbled out. 'Fine. I feel fine. I feel very well, in fact. Better than I have for a long time. I've got energy. I don't feel tired and pathetic. I do feel a bit jittery and it's pretty hard to sleep. But hey, I wrote a 10,000 word essay overnight a couple of days ago.' I was proud of myself, though I had printed it out and handed it in without re-reading it, as usual. 'And I bought a piano accordian.'

'Can you play it?' he asked.

'Well no, not yet,' I said.

'Have you felt like this before?' he said, seriously.

'Sometimes, I guess. Not nearly often enough! It's great.'

He asked a few more questions and then said I should come back for another appointment in two days' time. I didn't understand it, I was feeling well for once. Why would he want to see me again so soon?

'Just humour me, Vic,' he said patiently.

'Okay, just for you, but only because I'm such a nice and obliging patient.' And with that, I stood up and walked out.

The following week, I was back in Dr G's office.

'So how are you?' he asked.

'Okay.' There was silence for a while, as I dug my fingernails into my arms, not looking at him.

'How were you last week?' he continued.

'I had a lot of energy. A lot more than now.' I looked down at my faded black jeans and the black men's boots I'd bought second-hand at a market. I sighed.

'And does that kind of burst of energy happen a lot?' he asked.

'No, not a lot. Sometimes. It's a bit like being on speed I guess. People say that my voice changes. Peter says that I'm irritating when I'm upbeat – like an Energizer bunny you can't turn off. When he first told me that, I wouldn't speak to him for a month.' I smiled. 'I was really hurt. It was the first time in ages that I'd felt good, and all he could say was that I was annoying. And brittle, he said I seemed brittle.'

He then asked me if I'd ever had any periods when I thought I was invincible, or when I thought I had special powers. That I could fly, for instance. Had I ever thought I was someone powerful?

'You mean have I ever had a psychotic episode?' I said. 'Not as far as I know. I'm as sane as you are.'

He gave me a wry smile before asking about my thoughts.

I wasn't sure where he was going with this, so I chose my next words carefully. 'Sometimes I do find that I have a lot of thoughts at once, that they tumble out over one another. It coincides with the times I have a lot of energy. I don't always feel better, some-times just really twitchy.'

'Is there a reason you haven't mentioned this before?' He raised his eyebrows and looked at me over the top of his glasses. 'It's important.'

There were so many things I hadn't told him: how was I to know which were important? 'I'd forgotten, I guess. Besides, it doesn't bother me the way the other things do. My problem is self-harm.'

'I don't agree. That's just one of your problems.' He then explained that he thought it would be useful for me to try taking a drug called Lithium. It was used to control mood swings, particularly in bipolar disorder, or what used to be known as manic-depression. He scribbled out a prescription. I was to take it in addition to the Prozac. Since the Stelazine episode, I hadn't been prescribed any other medication. When I looked doubtful he explained that Lithium had been used to treat mania and depression for a long time, successfully. It was a salt that was already found naturally in small quantities in the body. He thought I suffered from the occasional manic episode but agreed with me that it was currently the depression that was causing my problems. Nevertheless, he didn't think the mood swings were helping.

'I think this is worth a try. What do you think?' Dr G then asked.

'Do I have a choice? I've evidently got a problem. I don't know how to deal with it so I'm going to hope that you know what you're doing.' I then added, 'As long as it won't do me any harm'.

He shook his head and told me the main side effect was that it makes you thirsty. I would also need to have a blood test every three months to monitor my levels. The main thing was to take the prescribed amount.

If it was harmless, why would I need a blood test? I wondered. But at least I now had a label for my condition. I couldn't see how this explained the self-harm but it didn't matter. Now when people asked what was wrong with me, I could say, 'It's manic-depression' rather than, 'I sometimes get this inexplicable urge to cut myself with razor blades'. This diagnosis was also confirmation that my condition wasn't my fault: I was sick.

Chapter Seven

Weeks later, I sat in Dr G's office and began to cry. I couldn't stop. I was taking my medication, I was attending lectures, I wasn't drinking, I was getting enough exercise and I wasn't even seeing Alex. Yet this wasn't enough. I was constantly tired, slow and sick of desperately trying not to hurt myself.

Dr G had me readmitted to the Clinic that evening.

In hospital you don't have to cook, clean, wash up, answer the phone, or even open your mail. You don't have to deal with everyday life. But you do have to be considerate of other patients, you have to eat dinner at what feels like mid-afternoon, and you also have to attend group therapy sessions. I knew from my previous stay that these didn't work for me.

The main problem with the therapy groups at N_ was that they were attended by a large number of people with different problems who were both self-obsessed and lacking insight. I was one of them. I used to sit there either thinking about other things, or alternating between wanting to talk and wanting the others to stop talking. These groups were exhausting, and, as I didn't believe I could benefit from them, I didn't. Who cared about anger management and dealing with anxiety? Certainly not me.

As I was ostensibly in hospital in order not to injure myself, I agreed to sign a contract again. I was confident that I could argue my way out of being scheduled, should I accidentally 'slip up'.

The nurse carried out a rather haphazard check of my belongings and then left me alone to unpack. I put away my socks and T-shirts. Took out my shoes and put them on the floor under my bed. I left the razor blade where I'd originally hidden it, at the bottom of my bag.

As the days passed, I became more and more tempted by the thought of the razor, and how easy it would be to use it. I was frustrated that I still wasn't getting any better, and I had way, way too much time on my hands.

There really was little to do beyond attending a couple of hours of group therapy or individual sessions each day, eating, smoking and watching dull TV in the common room. I wasn't able to read properly, so spent a lot of time either chatting to people or flicking through the pages of glossy magazines. This time, I also spent a lot of time lying on my bed staring at the ceiling, trying to decide if I should use the blade or not. The trouble was, it was there. As the weeks began to run into each other, I became more and more obsessed with it. The world shrank. Soon there was just the institution, the routines and a small razor blade at the bottom of an old overnight bag in the cupboard by my bed.

One quiet afternoon I retrieved it. My hands trembling, I walked slowly to the closest bathroom – I didn't want to stain the carpet – and carefully unwrapped the new blade. Cleanliness had become increasingly important, as I didn't want an infection, so after that initial trial with the breadknife, I only ever used fresh blades.

I felt an odd mixture of dismay and excitement. The reason I was in hospital was to avoid doing this. It had been explained very clearly to me that if I felt tempted, it was my responsibility to talk to one of the nurses. The trouble was, I knew this didn't help. Because I didn't really understand what I was doing I couldn't talk about it. I couldn't get beyond the very basic, 'I want to cut myself'. It was this inexpressible gulf between what I did, what I thought, and what little I could put into words, that made things so much more difficult.

I pulled the razor across my wrist and for a minute I just watched as the flesh opened up and the dark red blood began to leak out. It didn't matter if it was deep: I was already in hospital. If I miscalculated they would probably have found me before it was too late.

I then wrapped my arm in a towel and walked calmly out to the nurses' station. 'I've cut myself,' I said.

A rather tough older woman was on duty and she looked at me impassively. 'Let me see that.' As I unwrapped my forearm, she added, 'You're on a contract, aren't you Vic?'

I hadn't forgotten I was on a contract but suddenly felt nervous. What if they decided to schedule me? The other girl had been scheduled for just scratching her arms – she hadn't smuggled in a weapon and then used it. Fuck. I hadn't miscalculated how hard I needed to press to cut my arm but perhaps I had misjudged the hospital's likely response to my action. It finally occurred to me that the contract wasn't just about protecting me. What if someone else had found my razor?

The news of what I'd done travelled quickly around the ward. Soon I was sitting on my bed, holding my roughly bandaged wrist, surrounded by other patients. We were all waiting to hear what was going to happen to me. Everyone spoke quietly, offering a range of opinions.

'I don't see that they have a choice: you've broken your contract and you obviously shouldn't go home. They've got to schedule you.' This was from a doctor who had been suffering from severe depression but didn't know it until she began to cry hysterically, for no reason, in front of one of her patients.

'But you won't cope. State mental hospitals aren't like this place. I know, I've been in several of them.' And this woman was trying to be supportive?

'How are you feeling?' It was Annabel. Like me, she had been out for a while but was back.

I wasn't feeling good. The thought of a violent, cold and harsh place, in which I could be held against my will, was terrifying. But what really hurt was that I was completely responsible for putting myself in this position. For the first time I realised that this wasn't a game and that I probably couldn't talk my way out of it. No matter how rational I was able to sound, the evidence was against me.

It took an hour or so for them to locate Dr G – they didn't want to make a decision without discussing the matter with him. He couldn't come in so spoke to the nurse on the phone. He didn't ask to speak to me.

When I heard what the decision was I was stunned.

Everyone else was equally horrified.

'What will you do? Will you be okay?'

'Don't go home; go and stay with someone.'

'They're insane. This is ridiculous. They can't kick you out.'

But they could, and they did. They asked me to pack my bag and leave immediately. I sat there blinking away tears. I couldn't believe it. I had just been expelled from a psychiatric hospital.

They didn't explain the reasoning to me, but Dr G had no doubt calculated that as I'd done a fair bit of damage I was unlikely to do any more harm to myself for the next few days. He would also have known that a public hospital wouldn't have done me any good. His role wasn't to hand out punishments but to work out a suitable treatment plan. At the time, his actions just seemed callous.

First, I tried calling Catherine. She wasn't there. I then tried Peter but only got through to his answering machine. There was no-one else I could ask, as no-one else knew I was in hospital. I didn't have enough money for a taxi so had no choice but to walk to the train station, with my overnight bag over my shoulder and wrist roughly bandaged. The nurse had done that much. The one thing I wasn't going to do was cry.

When I arrived back at the flat the answering machine flashed at me from the kitchen table.

Needing to hear the sound of a human voice, I checked the messages. There was one from Peter.

'Hi Vic, can you call me as soon as you get this? I rang the hospital and they said you'd left and they weren't sure where you were. Are you all right? Silly question really. Anyway, I don't think you should be by yourself. So please call me when you get in.'

I called Peter back and half an hour later he turned up. He'd borrowed someone's car. 'Pack enough things for at least a week. I really don't think you should be here at the moment.' He came upstairs and looked around my room. 'Is there anything you want to give me?'

I went to my desk where I'd put the packet of razors.

'What brand are they this time?' he said, before I handed them over.

I told him they were Gillette, that there didn't seem to be much else on the market. He put them in his backpack to take home. Peter didn't like safety razors, as they gave him a rash, so was happy to have my cast-offs. Or so he said.

Next I asked if we could visit a medical centre. My wrist, which was now really hurting, needed some attention.

'Sure, but why didn't they do it at the hospital?' Peter looked surprised.

'Punishment? I don't know. They didn't say. Or maybe they did and I don't remember.'

Once at the medical centre, I didn't explain much to the doctor. It was too complicated. I had Peter with me so he didn't ask any questions. Just sewed it up.

Peter watched at the beginning, and then had to be helped out of the room. When I found him afterwards he was sitting down sipping a glass of water, his face a pale green-grey colour.

A little while later, we arrived back at Peter's college. The first thing he did was listen to his messages. There was one from a voice I recognised. I caught '. . . I can't believe what she's done now. When you've found her, would you mind calling me? I'd be most grateful.' The voice sounded tight: annoyed more than anything else, as though she were dealing with a frustrating child. To my mother I guess that's just what I was.

I was furious that she was talking to Peter like this. It was an invasion of privacy. Peter was my friend, what right did she have to bother him? I was also hurt. She didn't sound worried. Peter said I was misreading the message, that of course she was worried. He then called her back and assured her I was all right. I refused to talk to her myself. I couldn't.

I stayed with Peter and his brother Paul, who was on an extended holiday, at a male residential university college for two weeks. The three of us shared a large room, Peter had half the space, and Paul and I took a corner each. I used the communal bathrooms, but tried not to do so at the rush hour before lectures in the mornings, or after touch football games just before dinner in the evenings. At least the bathrooms had shower doors that closed, and separate loos, and they were cleaned daily. While I didn't actually eat with the boys in the dining room, they brought back meals for me. During the day, I went to the library and managed to do some research and reading, or visited people I knew. I felt fragile but for the first time in a while as though I were living a relatively normal life.

I wasn't, of course, and had to go home eventually.

Chapter Eight

A few days after I moved back to the flat, I was sitting downstairs in the kitchen eating dinner with Rodney when there was a loud crack and the lights went out.

We both rushed upstairs towards the source of the noise, and it was then that we saw the smoke. It was billowing out of Rodney's bedroom. One of his scented candles had fallen over, set the carpet alight and the flames had reached a cord, short-circuiting the power in the entire house.

We got things under control but the smell was appalling, and one corner of Rodney's room was destroyed. He packed his overnight bag and announced that he was going to stay with his girlfriend until the smell of smoke had gone. It was all very well for him.

I spent the next few days alone in the flat, hating it, hating the smell and hating Rodney. He wasn't thrilled with me either: I wasn't the person he'd hoped I'd be when we first met. It was time to move again. While browsing through the shared accommodation section of the *Herald*, I saw an ad for a room in a warehouse: 'suitable for use as a studio or as accommodation'. It sounded intriguing, and it would be great to have a chance to paint. Even though I'd dropped out of art school, painting and drawing were what I was happiest doing. (Not that I'd been doing much of either while at college.)

Rodney seemed surprised when I said I was leaving, but I'd made up my mind – and I'd put down a deposit.

The warehouse was a large building that had once been used for wool storage. It had two floors, a gallery space and internal walls made of particle board. The kitchen and bathrooms were concrete and primitive. My space was upstairs with a large window overlooking the road. I'd never had such a big room, so didn't care that the walls didn't reach the ceiling. Annabel visited, and looked around silently for quite a while. Finally, she stamped her foot, 'At least the floor seems solid'. My cousin who was in town for a few days, declared the place a fire hazard.

I loved it.

On my first night, one of my new housemates, Simon, invited everyone – there were ten of us at that stage – into his bedroom for a smoke. As I sat on a cushion on the floor, listening to everyone talk, I thought, this is going to be fun – I've done the right thing. The other people seemed interested, interesting, and unusually open. Some had known each other before moving in, while others knew the landlord. Only two of us had answered the ads in the paper.

Simon looked about seventeen but must have been older than that, as he already had a successful career as a photographer, judging by the many framed magazine spreads on the walls. Almost without preamble, he told us his history: abusive parents, teenage drug use, prostitution, and then a boyfriend who'd saved him, and introduced him to art. I was astonished by his frankness and relieved by it. Keeping secrets was so exhausting – perhaps I wouldn't have to do it here.

Ian sat next to me. I knew nothing about him, but he'd accused me that morning of being stuck-up. I had, he said, a posh accent, and was too polite. I'd obviously had it easy, according to him. 'So what's your story?' Ian asked. 'What are you doing here?'

I told them my recent history. I talked about the mental hospital and the fact, rather than the act, of self-mutilation. And I told them about the manic-depression label. It helped to explain why I wasn't doing the same thing as all my friends, why I wasn't working, why I wasn't living in a flat in the eastern suburbs and throwing dinner parties, and why I was now living in a dirty unheated warehouse.

The people in Simon's room found what I told them difficult to believe. They hadn't picked it. Apparently, the fact that I was able to talk cheerfully and smile a lot meant that I didn't look like the sort who'd want to harm herself. I didn't fit their stereotypes of wayward teenage girls, prison inmates and traumatised refugees. I seemed too normal.

Ian actually challenged me and suggested that I was making it up. He wanted to see evidence.

While my fresh and healing wounds mesmerised me, I was uncomfortable looking at my scars. The idea of displaying them worried me even more; they were private marks. The room was silent, as everyone looked at me, waiting to see what I'd do and, no doubt, wanting to see them. I'd noticed before that people had a morbid curiosity about them, and as a result I tried to keep them covered.

I considered telling Ian to fuck off, but they'd all see the scars sooner or later. I wasn't going to be able to get away with long sleeves all summer so it was probably easier to just do it now. I pulled up my sleeve to reveal the haphazard lines. Some of them were still surrounded by pink dots, where the stitches had been taken out.

My new housemates immediately said that I had to stop doing it, and that, while I was living there, I was to tell them if I felt as though I wanted to. They didn't treat me like I was mad. As I pulled my sleeve back down it seemed as if, maybe, it would all be okay.

I quickly settled in. There was always someone around, as most people at the warehouse didn't have a job. And they were friendly. There was always someone with whom you could go drawing, or to the pub, the movies or a café. We shared meat-free, wallet-friendly meals, and organised rosters for cleaning. The latter were good in theory, but the guys tended to ignore them, so the bins overflowed regularly and the showers were usually covered in mould. Maintaining any kind of normal hygiene levels was a challenge, but it must have been good for my immune system, as for the entire time I was there I wasn't sick.

Moving into the warehouse had been about more than changing my address: I'd moved into a different way of life. I was surrounded by people who weren't trying to succeed, who weren't competing and who were content to drift, and it was refreshing. I could stop trying so hard. As I wasn't eligible for a student allowance, the sporadic gallery pay wasn't enough to live on and I didn't want to waitress, I signed up for the dole. It was something I never thought I'd do, but then I hadn't known anyone who was on it. I did now.

Jade and Leigh, a hippie couple, often had friends over. They'd sit around and chat, drink and smoke for hours. And then, quite often, go clubbing. Wherever they went they always invited the rest of us to join them. Given that I'd now completely broken with everyone I knew, I invariably accepted the offers.

Clubbing was something I'd not ever done before, but I took to it quickly. It was a chance to dance and to dress up. As a result of months of not eating much, I had lost a lot of weight. Alice, a fashion student who had the room closest to me, was curvy and very con-scious of it. She couldn't believe that I only wore jeans and oversized T-shirts, anything, as long as it covered me up. Finally, as a result of her niggling, and Simon's, I bought some tartan hipster hotpants for a dollar at a market. They were both loudly impressed.

'I'd kill for legs like yours,' said Alice.

I couldn't believe it. I'd spent years agonising about my weight, hiding my body, and being ashamed of what I looked like – except for the rare brief periods when my mood was so upbeat I just had to show off. And now someone was jealous of my legs.

It made me brave enough to do something I'd always wanted to do: cut off my hair. For years it had been mousy brown and either chin or shoulder length. The most daring change I'd made was to have it streaked. My mother hated the look of girls with short hair. It was butch. I also worried about having so much of my face on view. With short hair you can't hide.

With each snip, I kept thinking I'd made a big mistake, but it was too late. I just had to sit there and look at my nervous face in the mirror. 'Trust me,' the hairdresser said, 'it'll be great. You've got lovely features. You'll feel a different person when I've finished with you.'

And I did. I looked and felt very different. I felt fresh, somehow, and clean. As I walked home, I kept stopping to look at my reflection. It didn't look like me – and that was very liberating. I was finally happy with the way I looked, with where I was living and with my new friends. For the first time in over a year, I didn't want to hurt myself.

But there were some things that I couldn't change: I still didn't trust men. I didn't hate them, but didn't trust them. My solution was to beat them at their own game, to become the girl who didn't want a relationship, who was happy to have a fling. It was less humiliating than getting attached to someone, only to find they were not interested in anything other than my body. Or to be more precise, sex. By keeping my expectations very, very low, I was able to avoid feeling – well, anything.

For months I existed quite happily in that strange limbo, without responsibilities, cut off from the world. I don't know how long I would have stayed if I'd been given the choice, but I wasn't. It was my body that rebelled first.

I was smoking dope in the warehouse one evening, which I did very rarely, as I knew it wasn't good for my mood. I began to feel odd. Not paranoid, but tense. It felt as though my muscles were about to go into spasms. Remembering the Stelazine incident only too clearly, and terrified that it would happen again, I asked one of my housemates to drive me to the local hospital. He volunteered to stay but I sent him home. If I was going to have convulsions, I didn't want them to be seen by anyone I knew.

Maybe the problem was that I'd been mixing Lithium, Prozac and grass. Or it might have been that the dope had been laced with something else. I had no way of knowing.

Once in the emergency ward, I was given an injection to calm me down. As I lay on the bed, I chatted to my friend Emily who was perched on top of a cupboard, next to the fish tank. We'd been inseparable at school, but I hadn't seen her for a long time, as she'd been living overseas. She'd been worried about me, she said, and had heard that I'd not been well. I told her not to worry. I was fine. Couldn't she see that?

It was several hours before it became evident that there was no cupboard, no fish tank and, most disappointingly, no Emily. I was in a hospital bed with the sides up and the curtains pulled around me.

Eventually I was told that I could leave, but only if someone collected me. I called Nicola, a very straight, conservative friend in her final year at law school. I don't know why I chose her. We'd not spoken for over a year and she had no idea where I'd been in the meantime. Despite this, and the fact that it was midnight, she turned up with her flatmate and suggested I stay the night with them. I insisted that I couldn't do so without my toothbrush.

As we were approaching her house, I reminded her that we had to collect the toothbrush.

'No, we don't Vic. It's in your hand.'

It was. We'd already been past the warehouse, I just had no memory of doing so.

Both of them admitted the next day that they were worried about me: the warehouse wasn't a good place.

Perhaps not, I said, but I had no intention of leaving. I did give up smoking dope, however, and kept my drinking to a minimum, despite Angus. A heavy-drinking Scot, Angus was the latest addition to our little community. His accent was impenetrable but I didn't care: he was beautiful. Long-haired, smooth-chested and tanned, he looked as though he'd walked off a Calvin Klein poster, not a building site.

We'd all been drinking vodka at the kitchen table one night, listening to someone's plan for a new sport involving horses and balls. Angus had only just arrived, and I didn't know him but by the end of the night we found ourselves alone in the kitchen. As I opened the fridge door, he saw the scars on my wrist.

'Bad habit,' was my response when he asked about them. He then pulled up his own sleeve and showed me a faded gash on his forearm. It had seemed like a good idea, he said, when he was sitting in a pub in Glasgow, high on magic mushrooms.

It was a bond, of sorts.

We started having what I thought of as an extended fling, not a relationship. He was happy enough for people to know we were seeing each other, but he had a 'real' girlfriend living in Melbourne. Only I knew this, and tried not to think about it. I focused on the fact that he liked me enough not to be embarrassed that other people knew it. This was a new thing for me.

There was a downside. I could hardly understand a word Angus said, and what little I could decipher related mainly to football, or beer. He also admitted that he was wanted by the Scottish police, and had skipped the country. When I asked him what he'd done, he was evasive, 'It was an accident. I hit a police-woman.' I tried not to think about that too – until he gave me no choice.

We were walking back from a pub late one night and popped into the kebab shop for a snack. As we were heading out, Angus told me to wait there for a moment. I assumed he was going for a pee, so stood on the street corner eating my kebab, trying to look non-chalant. After a few minutes he hadn't come back, which was odd. After a few more, it occurred to me that he wasn't going to. I started walking home in the dark. The bastard, I thought, getting more annoyed and upset with each step.

Lights were on at home, and I heard voices. Raised voices. Darren, one of the less tolerant members of the household, was worked up about something. I didn't care what it was. He had regular fights with his part-ner, as well as the other blokes living in the warehouse. And he wasn't the only one. I'd heard yelling one morning and gone down to the bathroom to find Ralph, who was well over six foot, with his boot on a naked, prostrated Ian's neck. But this did sound differ-ent. I walked past the table where Darren and Ian were sitting, and they immediately turned on me.

'I can't believe what a fucking arsehole that boyfriend of yours is,' Darren spat at me.

'What's he done?' I asked, puzzled, but not surprised that Angus had annoyed someone else.

Ian took over. 'He turned up here about fifteen minutes ago,' he paused, as my jaw dropped, 'and rushed in, saying he'd nicked a car. He then asked if anyone wanted to go for a joyride.'

'The bastard.' I was furious.

'Oh no, that's not the good bit. We went outside with him and he showed us a van – Darren's van. He'd managed to nick Darren's van which was parked up on the street outside the pub.' He shook his head. 'Can you believe that? And he screwed up the lock and the ignition while he was breaking in and hot-wiring it.'

I couldn't believe it. I'd actually been ditched so he could nick a car. 'Where's he now?' I asked.

'Don't know. The prick's disappeared again. In my van.'

I decided that I didn't want to be around when Angus returned, so went to bed.

A few days later, as I watched Angus expertly kick down the door to Arthur the landlord's self-contained flat, I decided that it really was time to end it.

There had been a council inspection, prior to which we had been told to hide our beds. This odd request had led the guys to do some investigating and they had discovered that the warehouse was actually zoned light industrial, not residential. We were, therefore, living there illegally – and Arthur knew this. Furthermore, the guys had discovered that our rent, which was supposed to be funding improvements to the kitchen, bathroom and gallery space, was being channelled into one of Arthur's other businesses. He'd never had any intention of improving the place for us, which had always been the promise.

We knew something had been going on, as new partitions had been going up regularly, followed by ads in the paper for new tenants. There were now fourteen of us. We were all pissed off by what we'd discovered about Arthur, and decided to take over the lease for ourselves, as he wasn't actually the owner.

And then Arthur disappeared. Angus volunteered to break into his flat, to see if we could find out where he'd gone. There was nothing. No furniture, no food and no clues. The flat was empty.

A month or so later, just as we'd got used to squatting, a formal eviction notice turned up. We had a week to move, and I decided to go rather than wait to be escorted off the premises. I packed up my things and left.

I'd planned to stay in touch with everyone but by the time I had settled into my new flat and had the energy to call them, the phone had been cut off. I went to visit but the place was boarded up and vacant.

Chapter nine

After living in a household of fourteen people with only two showers to share, the idea of a place of my own was enormously appealing. I rented a one-bedroom ground floor flat that had once been part of a Victorian terrace house. It was the first affordable place I was offered. A tall thin bloke with lank hair lived upstairs.

The design was peculiar. A home conversion had been made, and what would once have been a front sitting room was now a small kitchen and dining room. By 'dining room' I mean there was space for a table and some chairs. A bookshelf divided this section from the bedroom and bathroom. The high ceilings and open spaces meant the flat was impossible to heat but I didn't care. It was mine.

It was wonderful to be able to do what I liked, when I liked, without regard for any housemates. I'd never had that kind of freedom before and it was amazing. And it was how I managed to overlook the hideous carpet, the damp and the weeds in the garden.

But while I loved the privacy, it wasn't exactly good for me.

At first I actually invited friends over, uni friends from whom I'd cut myself off over the last couple of years. I even cooked. But as the months passed, everything started to become more of an effort. When I went out, I tended to drink. Heavily.

One morning I woke up next to a bloke I hardly knew, and certainly hadn't seen for years. I had no memory of what had happened the previous night. I threw up, dressed and went to the gallery, telling him to let himself out. I'd never had such a complete blackout before, but had certainly slept with people inadvertently due to drinking too much.

Most of the time I just stayed home in the flat, watching television or reading. Occasionally I went into uni, where I was still studying. I began letting the phone ring out and stopped returning calls. There was something wrong but I didn't know what to do. The worse I felt, the more I thought I should keep away from people when I was like this: I didn't want to 'inflict' myself on them. The urge to hurt myself returned as well. Sometimes I gave in to it. It was easier than dealing with the thoughts, which would be all-consuming until I finally picked up the razor blade.

Dr G, who I still saw on a weekly basis, suggested another spell in hospital.

The idea of going in again appealed but I was worried about my studies. I didn't want to miss any seminars. Hospital stays could last weeks and that was too long. I'd never catch up. So I said no, I'd stay home and cope as best I could. Dr G didn't think this was a wise idea, so suggested a compromise: I could go to hospital and attend uni on special day release.

For some weeks then, every couple of days, I'd catch the train from the hospital to the campus. Neither place was directly on the railway line, so there was a walk at each end. As I was now on a sedative as well as Prozac and Lithium, this trip wasn't easy; I was constantly exhausted and each step was an effort. On the few times I arrived at the English department early, I'd collapse on the floor outside the seminar room and lie down, grateful to have even ten minutes' rest. I didn't care what people thought.

While I was able to force myself to attend seminars, I didn't enjoy them anymore. I couldn't concentrate. I couldn't follow what other people were saying and I couldn't understand the readings we were given. Nothing made sense. It was as though I were surrounded by a thick fog and I desperately wanted to escape it. The frustration grew to the point where, for the first time in my life, I began to feel violent-not just towards myself but others as well. I wanted to scream and throw chairs. I wanted to push tables over. I wanted to punch and kick and hit. But I didn't, instead I sat there with my jaws clenched, hour after hour, wondering what was next. I then did the only thing I could think of: I told my psychiatrist.

The obvious solution seemed to be to stop going to seminars and take the rest of the term off. But the truth was that I wasn't sure I was ever going to get better. Just giving up made no sense to me-I wasn't going to do that. University was the only stable thing in my life. Without it I would be adrift and that was a terrifying thought. There had to be another way. Perhaps,

I thought, I could change the way my degree was structured and instead of doing coursework, I could do a thesis or long essay. That way, I wouldn't have to be in a classroom.

The course coordinator agreed to see me, and I told him about my problem, about the drugs, the hospital, my desire to throw chairs, and my suggested solution. My psychiatrist had agreed to supply any medical certificates the university might need. The course coordinator listened carefully, then said it wasn't quite as simple as that. He would need to check my academic record and meet with several other members of the department before making a decision.

A week later, I was told that if I could come up with a suitable research topic and find a supervisor, then yes, I could complete the second half of my degree by writing a 30,000 word essay. All I had to do was find a topic and a supervisor. I chose Jackie Collins, transgression, and asked the head of the department to be my supervisor. She agreed, stipulating that I wasn't only to write about Jackie Collins' bonkbusters but to compare her work with that of a nineteenth century equivalent. I found one.

Home again, and feeling better, I winced when the owner of my flat cut down the only appealing feature of the entire property: the frangipani tree. I'd not complained when the bloke upstairs sold my bike to buy smack, nor did I leave when someone tried to climb in my bedroom window. (The bloke upstairs, perhaps feeling guilty about the bike, scared him off.) I tolerated the cold, the ugly orange tiles in the bathroom, the cramped conditions. It was the removal of the frangipani that did it.

It was time to move again.

Chapter Ten

It was time to live in a place I actually liked. The new flat was light, clean, had a luscious tropical garden, and was near the beach. For the first time since I'd lived in Sydney, I didn't trip over people asking for money whenever I walked out the door.

My parents, delighted that I was out of the inner city, decided not only to lend me furniture, but to buy me some. Instead of three chairs, a futon and an old table, I had two bright yellow sofas, a coffee table and a real bed, with a mattress. My desk looked out onto the balcony.

I wanted to invite people into my house, and back into my life.

I was still taking antidepressants and mood stabilisers but fewer tranquillisers now. So I didn't feel nearly as tired. No longer having to attend seminars meant that I could potter around the library when I felt like it, or work from home, or I could sit in a café and read. The choice was mine.

My hair, which had looked great when it had first been cut off, had over the months become straggly and out of shape. I'd dyed it myself several times, first red and then black, and I had to admit it looked awful. It was time for a professional to have a go at it. When it was cut, and back to its normal shade of light brown, it looked shiny and healthy.

And that was how I felt. Shiny and healthy.

And then I met Patrick.

I was 24, and still hadn't got the hang of how to deal with men. There'd been many one-night stands, there'd been Alex, and there'd been Angus. I knew that Alex had never loved me, but I'd always told myself it didn't matter. And I'd decided that I wasn't worth loving a long time before I got involved with Angus.

Patrick was, in fact, Alex's boss. We met late one night when I was having a drink with Alex. We'd finally stopped sleeping together and as a result were getting along much better, so Patrick was introduced to a relaxed version of me. We spent the night telling anecdotes, laughing and playing pool.

When Patrick called me the next day I was shocked. We'd got on well but I hadn't sensed that he was interested in me – and I wasn't used to blokes asking me out. My first thought was that perhaps it was a joke. He seemed too, too together to want to have anything to do with me.

I tried to sound indifferent and casual. Sure, I'd be happy to meet up. A drink perhaps?

No, he wanted me to come to dinner. He shared a house with two girls but they were going away for the weekend, so he'd have the kitchen, indeed whole house, to himself. As they also had a spa, I should bring my bathers.

It seemed ironic to me that just when I'd decided I'd rather be on my own than be the girl you have when you don't have a girlfriend, along came someone cute, funny and warm who seemed to be genuinely interested in me.

As the weekend approached, I tried not to get excited.

As I knocked on Patrick's door I felt nervous. He did seem a nice guy, but didn't nice guys like nice girls? I wasn't that. I wasn't even a normal girl. The scars flashed through my mind. I'd worn a long-sleeved T-shirt and jeans – my uniform – so he couldn't see them immediately, but what about the spa?

I was torn. I didn't want to show my scars but at the same time didn't want the fact of them to stop me doing things. If he suggested the spa, I'd go in, and if I had to explain, I would. I'd tell him I'd had a bizarre ice-skating accident and that it was too painful to discuss. Flashbacks and all that. Actually, Alex might have already told him about me – after all, he'd given him my phone number. But I doubted it. Alex was clearly still ambivalent about me but had never been malicious.

I had to assume Patrick knew nothing.

He opened the door, smiling, and the smell of cooking wafted down the stairs behind him. He offered me champagne. I didn't quite know what to do, so accepted a glass. And then another. He fiddled around in the kitchen and talked, and the more he talked, the more I drank. He was actually being nice to me and I couldn't cope with it. Drinking seemed the best way to deal with the problem.

And then the topic of the spa came up. Apparently, it was huge, and in the garden, and a wonderful thing to do in winter. Relaxed now, I thought it sounded like a good idea, and I changed into my bathers in his room.

The contrast between the air temperature and the water was wonderful, and for those first few moments in the spa I understood its appeal. And then I began to see tiny stars, and feel pins and needles in my hands and feet. I was about to faint.

Patrick managed to get me back to his bedroom, where I lay on top of his – increasingly damp – doona and watched the room swirl about me. It wasn't a good sign. As long as I don't throw up, I thought, and concentrated on not doing so.

Patrick came in with a glass of water, and sat on the end of the bed. What could he do to help? Anything? Would food improve things? He was being embarrassingly considerate. All I wanted was to be at home. I asked him to call me a taxi.

Things really hadn't gone well, and it was a pity. He really did seem nice. In a way I was relieved. He wouldn't call again and I wouldn't have to deal with all that a relationship entailed. It was better to be by myself.

The next day he rang. He apologised for the previous evening. It was his fault. He knew that champagne and spas didn't mix. Could he take me out to make up for it? To a restaurant. Nowhere near water.

The restaurant was fantastic. Patrick was a chef, so I let him order and talk me through the menu. I hadn't, until then, been aware of how little I knew about food. It had always been something to be wary of, something that would make me fat, or sick. At best it was something to give me enough energy to get out of bed. It wasn't something that I actually knew how to appreciate.

Patrick was interested in everything, and knowledgeable without being opinionated. We discovered a mutual admiration for *Blake's 7*, a creaky old BBC sci-fi drama. Patrick even knew a video store that stocked it on tape. I was beyond impressed.

After a few weeks, I began telling people I was seeing someone. I even told my parents.

'That's lovely, darling. So what does he do?' said my mother.

I told her the name of his restaurant, hoping that its reputation might help.

'Oh, a chef. That's nice.' It was evident from her tone that that wasn't nice at all. 'And what does he look like? Where did he go to school?' Was he, in other words, suitable?

Some chefs don't like to cook when they are off duty, but Patrick would arrive at my door, grocery bags under each arm. He wouldn't tell me what we were going to eat, but would instead pour me a glass of wine and order me out of the kitchen. Invariably, whatever he made was delicious, and I began to relax enough to actually enjoy tastes and textures. I turned my mental calorie counter off. Occasionally, if I asked very nicely, he'd let me watch as he prepared something impossibly complicated, but I wasn't allowed to do any work other than set the table. 'You've been studying,' he'd say, 'you need a break'.

I'd find chocolates hidden in drawers and cupboards after he left the following day.

Part of me kept expecting to find something
wrong with Patrick. I even tried to bait him, to get him
to show the dark, unpleasant side that had to exist. He
certainly smoked too much, and drank a lot. But these
were things with which I could cope. When Alex first
heard we were going out, he had phoned me to warn
me that Patrick had a coke habit, which even if it were
true – and if so he kept it well hidden – was a bit rich
coming from Alex, who maintained that the best sex
he'd ever had was with a tree, while on acid.

When Patrick saw my scars, he didn't ask about
them, or quickly change the topic. Instead he held out
his own arms, which were zigzagged with white lines.
'Oven burns from taking out trays. You'd be surprised
how many people assume I had a tough childhood.' He
laughed, and was more interested in what I was writing than the history of my mental health. As far as he
was concerned, what was important was that I was fine
now. And I was. I was more than fine. I was content.

He told me about his childhood in north
Queensland, where in the wet season his family's
mobile home had to be tied down so as not to live up
to its name. He told me about his birth, which happened at exactly the same time as man first landed on
the moon. As a result, he was a blue baby – the umbil-
ical cord had wrapped itself around his neck while
everyone was in front of a portable TV watching the
broadcast of Neil Armstrong making his historic walk.
In turn, I told him about my childhood: the farm
which I'd loved, the move to the city which I'd seen as
such an adventure, and then life at uni. I even told him

about the cutting and the depression. It seemed like a long time ago, even though it was only months since I'd last been in hospital. It felt like I was talking about a different person.

There was a problem, however. Patrick was planning to move back to Queensland. He'd told me the first time we met but I kept hoping he'd change his mind. There was no way I was going to suggest he stayed, that was up to him. But I hoped that maybe I'd be worth it.

As his departure date approached I grew increasingly tense. He talked about Brisbane, and was excited about the prospect of somewhere laid-back and warm, of a new job. He hadn't decided where. He'd wait until he arrived. He didn't talk about what would happen to our relationship, and he didn't use the word 'we'. Clearly this was a solo project – it always had been and I hadn't changed that. I hadn't been enough to change that.

So I broke up with him.

I didn't say I'd miss him, that I'd be lonely without him, or even say that I really cared about him. Instead I lied. I told him that going out with someone and studying at the same time was too difficult. He was too much of a distraction. I wished him well in Queensland. He looked surprised but didn't argue, and that's what really hurt. I'd taken a gamble and lost; all I was left with was his Christmas present. Candlesticks.

Alex rang a few days later, saying he'd heard I'd broken up with Patrick.

'Was he upset?' I asked.

'No. Not really. More puzzled, I'd say.' I could always count on Alex for honesty when I didn't want it. 'He thought things were going well.'

'They were,' I said. 'They were going very well. That wasn't what it was about.' Alex wasn't the person to hear that I didn't want to be the one left. That I was just getting in before Patrick did. That Patrick had been the first bloke who'd cared when my birthday was, who really cared about me. I hung up.

At first I managed pretty well. I tried not to think about Patrick. I tried to keep up with friends and I tried to write. As long as I keep busy, I thought, I'll get through.

Emily, the friend I'd once hallucinated back into my life, was now back in the country for real. While Peter and Catherine focused on my depression and the self-mutilation, Emily didn't. She didn't ignore it exactly, just didn't engage with it. To her, I was Vic, the same person she'd always known. Sure, I behaved in odd and disturbing ways from time to time, but didn't everyone?

She lived nearby with her boyfriend, and after I broke up with Patrick, I spent more and more time with them. But it wasn't enough.

The fact was, most of my days were spent sitting in front of a computer in a one-bedroom flat, and it was beginning to get to me. I was still trying to work out an argument and it was proving difficult. I'd had it for a while, but ideas are slippery things, and I couldn't quite grasp it now.

Then, like a virus that never really leaves but goes into remission, just waiting for a chink in your immune system, the images and urges began to come back. Maybe pain would sharpen my thoughts. Wake me up. And if not, it was an appropriate punishment for my stupidity. I was stupid, stupid, stupid, I told myself. It didn't occur to me that the medications I was taking might be making things more difficult or that I was more upset about Patrick than I wanted to admit. And that it was affecting my ability to work.

Instead I struggled on, writing what I could when I could. When it all became too hard, I went to bed, no matter what time of day it was. Sleeping was better than giving in to the urge to hurt myself, no matter how much I believed I deserved it. I desperately didn't want to get dragged back into that pattern. The razors, the scars, the stitches, the hospitals. I wouldn't do it.

Eventually, I managed to write something that seemed to make sense. My supervisor had seen sections of it but as she put it, I was 'circling'. I certainly had something but it wasn't focused yet. I kept working, eventually producing the required number of words. If it was accepted, I'd get my Master's. If not – I wasn't going to think about that. I couldn't read back over it and tie up all the loose ends, and make sure it made sense, because I was afraid I would destroy it instead. By not checking my draft, I was protecting it, and, as a consequence, myself. I'd become so paranoid about my inability to write coherently that I couldn't read over what I'd written. It wasn't the first time this had happened, but it was the worst possible timing. This was an English literature thesis after all: it was supposed to be at least coherent and well written, if not wonderfully original.

Emily, Dee (another friend from the past) and my mother all agreed to look at the long essay or thesis – whatever it was – and happily pointed out the spelling errors and non sequiturs, while also being very encouraging. So, buoyed briefly, I included their sug-gestions, while being careful not to read any complete sentences. Then I printed it out and handed in three bound copies for marking, as required.

I had expected to feel excited at finishing. After years of study I was finally free and I didn't have to feel guilty if I wasn't reading or taking notes or working on a chapter. I should have been delighted, but instead I felt flat and lost. I now had to get a job but couldn't imagine who would employ me. I'd already sent off my resumé to various companies and those that had both-ered to respond had said they had nothing available. All of the jobs advertised in the paper asked for expe-rience. I had some, as I'd had a number of part-time jobs over the years, but waitressing, dressmaking, tutoring, and shopkeeping didn't seem to be of any use, unless you wanted a job in those areas. I didn't.

It was obvious what I had to do.

I went to the local chemist and bought a packet of razor blades. Then I sat down at the dining room table and put a towel carefully under my right wrist, feeling strangely detached. It had been a while, but I remem-bered the sequence. I put the blade to my flesh, brac-ing myself.

It was bad, though I had once again avoided doing any serious damage. What Annabel in the Acute Ward had once said was true, 'Arteries are surprisingly slippery'. She went searching for them from time to time, so was in a position to know.

The nearest doctor's surgery was about five minutes away by car, but fifteen on foot. As I wasn't able to drive and hold together the cut at the same time, I walked. I felt better as I headed up the hill towards the shops, but disappointed in myself. It had been over six months since I'd last done this, and I thought I was over it. That I'd escaped.

The doctor, who I'd not seen before, made little comment. As he tended my forearm, I looked at the framed photographs of his family on the walls of the surgery, and wondered what he thought of me. Whatever it was, he didn't think I was either insane or in danger, and he didn't ask what the problem was. Sighing, he asked if I was seeing a psychiatrist regularly, and asked for his name. And that was it. Sixteen stitches later I was allowed to go home. Did he believe that no matter what he said, I'd just keep cutting?

When I got home there was a message for me. An academic looking for a research assistant wanted to see me. It was just the kind of work I could do; it was perfect.

Two days later, my arm neatly bandaged, I went to the interview wearing my most conservative clothes: a striped long-sleeved shirt, cream pants and navy loafers. The sort of clothes a reliable person would wear. My arm ached a little as I drove across town. Even though my mother had warned me the evening before that the job market was tough, that for every one job there were a hundred applicants and that I should be prepared not to get it, I was optimistic.

The interview was at the woman's house, a small terrace smelling of damp. She worked from home, so that's where the job would be based. The pay would be hourly, and she envisaged needing someone about two days a week. I should know, she said, that she'd already seen two people who'd be perfect. She wasn't going to score the trifecta that day. Not with me, I knew that immediately. As we talked I became less and less confident in my ability to do anything at all.

As I drove home, weeks, months, of pent-up frustration began to surface. Hurting my arm hadn't been enough; I'd known that at the time. But what else was there?

Staring straight ahead, I put my foot on the accelerator. There was a crash and my car – or rather my mother's car – concertinaed, the front disappearing completely. The impact left me shaken and bruised, but not bleeding.

The vehicle in front of me was hardly damaged, and, as I quickly discovered, belonged to a paramedic. He rang an ambulance, and then calmly helped me out of the wreck.

Initially, I was X-rayed to check for broken ribs. The lead belt fell low around my hips. 'Not much of you, is there?' said one of the nurses cheerfully. I had hardly noticed as the kilos had dropped off. It was ironic; once I had believed that a body this size was all you needed to be happy.

When the police officers came in, I was lying on a bed in emergency. There were two of them, each asking questions. What time had the accident occurred? What kind of car did I drive? Could they see my licence? Could I describe what had happened? Had I done it on purpose?

It was possible that they'd seen my patient file, as I'd been in this hospital once before. My sleeves were rolled up though, so perhaps they'd just seen my bandaged forearm and jumped to their own conclusions.

Had I done it on purpose? It was a fair question, all things considered. I didn't know but I certainly wasn't going to tell anyone else that. I had to be very, very careful about what I said now. If I admitted to anything other than a lapse of concentration, I'd probably get scheduled and charged with negligent driving. As it was, both of these things were already on the cards. 'I don't know how it happened; it was just an accident,' I said. And apologised.

They left me alone for a few minutes and then returned. I was shaking. 'We're going over your side of town, do you want a lift home?'

I'd got away with it. Again.

Once back home, I rang Emily and told her what had happened. There was a pause, and then the sound of laughter. 'How do you do it?' She was right. Things were getting farcical. But she wasn't callous and quickly added, 'Are you all right?'

There was nothing broken. My shoulder, ribs and hips were bruised from the seatbelt, my knees were bruised from hitting the bottom of the dashboard. Other than that, I was surprisingly intact.

'How about we come over with some takeaway and a video?'

I thought of saying no, that wasn't necessary, but then changed my mind. I began to tidy up the flat, but didn't get further than emptying the ashtrays. Emily and her boyfriend would cope. The only person who really cared about tidiness was the owner of the car, my mother.

I rang her next. 'As long as you are all right, that's all that matters. The car's insured, I can get another. I'll be in town the day after tomorrow, so we can sort out things then.'

Two days later, my mother arrived to collect me. We had to go to the wrecker's yard to look at the damage and fill in the insurance forms. The first thing she noticed was my bandaged arm.

'What happened there?'

I tried to sound convincing. 'It was in the accident. There was something near the steering wheel.' I shook my head. 'I really don't remember.' I hoped that would be enough for her.

At the wrecker's one of the mechanics showed us what remained of the car. 'Like a sardine can, these things. You might as well be on a bicycle for all the protection they give you.' He patted the roof and smiled.

My mother was looking into the driver's side. 'So, which bit was it that cut your arm, dear?'

I looked in, trying to find something that might have done it. There was nothing. 'I don't know. Don't worry about it. It doesn't hurt,' I said, trying not to show her how much my discomfort increased with each new question.

She persisted. 'If it's bad enough to need a bandage, then we need to put it on the insurance claim form.'

'It doesn't matter. I'm fine.' Couldn't she just leave it alone?

Then the mechanic piped up. 'She's right, they like all those kinds of details. A nasty cut, was it?'

My mother finally turned away from the car and looked at me, then at my bandaged arm. Had she known all along that it was nothing to do with the accident? Her look of disgust and anger suggested that she'd suspected, but had wanted me to confirm it.

It was a look that I wanted to get away from – as far away as possible. I wanted to get away from her shame and my own guilt. I wanted to start afresh, somewhere else.

Chapter Eleven

The official story was that I was taking some time out. I was tired, that was the problem. I was going to South Australia to do a bit of photography, a bit of drawing, maybe have a go at writing a book. Maybe even get a job. Adelaide wasn't as fiercely competitive as Sydney, and I had relatives there. It would be a nice change.

The truth was that I was really scared. It wasn't just guilt but the fear of what I might do to myself if I stayed. I didn't believe that my psychiatrist could help me through this. It was something I had to do by myself.

Two weeks to the day after the accident, I got on a plane. My furniture was in storage and the keys to my flat had been handed in. I had only a suitcase, a small computer and a darkroom kit, the last a parting gift from Peter.

Initially I stayed with my aunt and uncle who were rattling around in a large, empty house as their four children had all left home. They let me use the back section, which had its own bathroom, bedroom and sitting room, and I got ready to settle into life in a new city. Used to people staying and doing their own thing, they left me alone. We ate meals together, and sometimes watched TV together, but that was pretty much it. They didn't ask why I was there, and I knew that my own parents wouldn't have told them.

At first I wasn't sure what I wanted to do, so, to fill in time, I wandered around the city taking photos. Perhaps, I thought, I could take portrait shots professionally. My cousin's children, who were perky and blonde, were happy to pose for me. When I developed the shots – in the back bathroom that I'd turned into a darkroom – I was disappointed. The children were cute but that didn't mean the photos were any good. Perhaps it wasn't the career for me.

But I didn't have to decide on one immediately as I was on sickness benefits, a form of social security, for three months. I had been on the dole, but that meant I had to apply for jobs regularly, and my psychiatrist had agreed that I needed a little break before going to my next job interview. In the meantime, I did want to make some more money, and to move toward supporting myself, while I wasn't under any pressure. Waitressing and bartending seemed like the only real options, when suddenly it occurred to me that there was something else I could do.

Something that didn't require any experience.

That was how I found myself in the front foyer of the North Adelaide School of Art, asking if they were looking for any life drawing models.

I loved life drawing myself, and it was one of the reasons I'd enrolled in art school in the first place. Of course I didn't think it would get me a job, so I had studied something called electronic and temporal art.

Or electric clockmaking, as some wit said. It was really film, TV, sound and animation, and, for my liking, too far removed from the physical creative process. What I liked was getting my hands dirty, and feeling charcoal on paper. And I could get so caught up in the geography of the human body that I'd forget myself. It was the only thing I'd ever done that I found completely absorbing – without being stressful. The models I most liked to draw were fat, very thin, or oddly shaped. They were the most interesting. Slim women were boring to draw. And that was the other reason I signed up to take my clothes off in front of a room full of students: I'd begun to hate my body again and I thought it might help.

After several years of being not just slim but often thin, I'd begun to put on weight again, and mysteriously, to develop acne on my back. The gym didn't appear to be working, and I had lost the ability to diet. Perhaps if I showed people my body in this way, I'd feel less ashamed, and just be able to deal with how I now looked.

They offered me the Wednesday afternoon class.

The following week I arrived fifteen minutes early and introduced myself to the teacher. As I took my clothes off I took a deep breath and told myself that I was being paid for this, and they weren't judging my body. It was just a shape to them; drawing me was an exercise.

The first pose was a standing one. Putting my hand on my hip, I tried to remember the poses of some of the other models I'd seen. The main thing was to stay still and not to look embarrassed. The effort of doing both kept me busy until the break. I was relieved when it came, as I was stiff and keen to put on my dressing gown. I also wanted to look at what they had drawn. Who they had drawn.

It was an unnerving feeling, seeing so many pictures of myself, some with different proportions, all with different styles. I was drawn to several that made my thighs look bigger, emphasising their curves and pushing down on the charcoal until they appeared heavy and solid. This attraction surprised me until I realised that it was exactly the way I would have drawn them and it turned them into the feature you wanted to hold, rather than hide.

Everyone should do life drawing I thought, as I walked home that afternoon. Then maybe they'd understand why women didn't all need to be thin. I hoped it was a thought I'd be able to keep.

Around this time, I also decided that I should see a GP – just to check in, really. I felt fine but knew that things could change, and it was best to be prepared. The GP referred me to a local psychiatrist, Dr C. I didn't really want to go, but, nevertheless thought our first meeting went well.

After the appointment he wrote the following letter to my new doctor.

20/6/95

Dear Dr X,

RE: Victoria Leatham

Thank you for referring this 26 year old woman for an assessment of her Bipolar Disorder and behavioral problems. Victoria currently lives with her aunt and uncle having returned from living in Sydney two months ago. She is currently on unemployment benefits but does some part-time work in photography or dressmaking. In the past she has attended university and has a Masters degree in English Literature.

Victoria gave a history of psychiatric disturbance since at least the age of 12 years. During her teenage years she principally had problems with anorexia nervosa but was also involved in episodes of self harm during these years. Subsequent to this time she has gradually come to have fluctuating episodes of Major Depression as well as occasional episodes of mania. Throughout both of these times she has tended to harm herself by cutting her arms or legs with a razor and has also had episodes of auditory hallucinations at times. In the past 3 years she has had three admissions to . . . in Sydney and has been seeing one psychiatrist consistently over the past 2 years for supportive psychotherapy. Although Victoria also gave a history of past abuse of alcohol, marijuana and amphetamines she denied using any of these substances for at least two years.

Victoria's development is characterised by her being raised in a family where everyone seemed to criticise her except her father who seemed to rather ignore her. Even her brothers thought that 'I'm a waste of space' and teased her repeatedly. In her early life this family environment was balanced out by her being brought up on a farm and being able to escape from the family. In addition, she was an intelligent young girl who was able to perform quite well at school. Unfortunately, at the age of 11 her parents lost the farm . . . and the family had to move to [the city]. Victoria found the entrance into a large high school to be quite overwhelming for her. Her life since this time has been characterised by episodes of severe psychiatric illness interspersed with periods of relatively good functioning. However, she has never been able to maintain any sustained relationships through these years.

At interview, Victoria presented as a rather evasive and anxious woman who clearly seemed to wish that she was not with me. She did not present as depressed or as manic but her thinking patterns were illogical at times.

The history and presentation are consistent with a diagnosis of Bipolar Disorder upon a background of multiple other problems. These include probable Borderline Personality Traits, an eating disorder in remission, and a family background of severe dysfunction. In addition, she has very little in the way of social supports or a sense of structure or organisation to her life.

I have encouraged Victoria to continue with her same medication for the time being. This consists of Lithium carbonate 750mg per day as well as Prozac 40mg daily. I will see if I can engage her further in some therapy and would hope to give her a mixture of problem oriented psychotherapy and supportive psychotherapy. We have arranged to meet on a further 2 or 3 occasions and Victoria will decide if she wishes to continue to see me at that time. I will let you know of her progress.

Yours sincerely

I was shocked.

It was a letter that made my family sound awful and me sound mad.

My brothers were mean and my parents were busy. Was that so dysfunctional? And there were mistakes. I didn't cut myself as a teenager, and I only once cut myself on my leg. And auditory hallucinations? I'd been misinterpreted in this way before when trying to explain to a psychiatrist about my inner voice.

The rest, however, was pretty accurate. His description of this Victoria – this troubled, neurotic person – suddenly made it clear to me why my family and friends found me so difficult to understand. And why they were so worried about me.

Chapter Twelve

One of the reasons I'd decided to go to South Australia was our family beach house. Built in the 1950s, the only alterations it had undergone since then were the addition of an overhead fan in the sitting room and a phone in the kitchen. Sitting at the top of a cliff, it was a house I'd known well as a child when each summer my mother would pack up the car with towels, bathers, cricket bats, tennis balls, sunburn cream and hats, and we'd head off. My father didn't usually come, as it was bushfire season.

When the life drawing course finished, I decided it was time to go down there.

As soon as I walked in, I was greeted by a familiar, musty smell, and I wondered why I hadn't thought of going to the house sooner. I spent the afternoon opening cupboards, looking at the bookshelves and sliding old suitcases filled with children's games out from under beds.

When night fell, I found something I hadn't counted on: silence. There were no neighbours and little traffic. It was just me. Alone.

As I made scrambled eggs in the kitchen that had always been filled with siblings fighting, or whinging, or flicking each other with tea towels, I felt apprehensive but couldn't put my finger on why. Perhaps I just needed background noise. There was an old black and white television in the back bedroom cupboard. As far as I knew it hadn't ever been used for anything but watching cricket matches, but it would do. I put it on a side table and adjusted the antenna. It worked.

After three days, during which I'd visited the local supermarket, walked down to the beach several times, read a bit and watched a bit of TV, I felt an increasing need to talk to someone else. I knew only one other person in the area.

I'd been walking my aunt's – very large – Alsatian one day, and had seen a photography exhibition advertised. I'd tied up the dog outside the hall where the exhibition was being shown, and went inside. As soon as I was out of sight, the dog began to bark, and bark, and bark. Reluctantly, I was about to untie him and take him home, when a girl approached me. She introduced herself as Mandy and asked if I wanted her to look after the dog while I looked at the pictures. It was an offer too good to refuse, so I left her patting him, and went back in.

As I was wandering around inside, a man came up to me. He was Mike, Mandy's father. They'd both been watching me with my dog, he said, and he'd suggested that Mandy should offer to help. We chatted for a few minutes, and I discovered that he had a house in the same small coastal town as our family. He said that I must get in touch when I next came down for a visit.

When I phoned, Mike immediately remembered who I was, and asked about the dog. Then he asked me to dinner the following night. I was taken aback, but nevertheless accepted the invitation.

It had been a while, quite a while, since I'd been out, so I decided to dress up for the occasion. No-one knew me here so I could wear and do what I liked. I put on a green suede miniskirt done up at the front with press-studs, stockings with very obvious black suspenders, knee-high boots, and a very low-cut black T-shirt. Everything was tight, though not by design. I'd bought the clothes during my flamboyant period at the warehouse.

Mike's eyes widened when I arrived but he didn't comment. Instead he poured me a glass of wine and talked nonstop as he chopped the vegetables. I didn't get a chance to say anything.

The house wasn't his, it belonged to a friend and he was just looking after it for a few months. He was 44 and divorced, and his daughter Mandy visited him on alternate weekends. He had a small business, selling cards, but he admitted it made no money and certainly didn't take up any time. In fact, he told me with surprising candour, he was essentially unemployed and not particularly interested in finding a job – he was more interested in having a lifestyle he enjoyed, and being happy.

This sounded good to me.

When he kissed me later that evening, I was surprised; when he suggested we go to bed I couldn't think of any reason not to. He was warm, funny and liked me.

From then on, I became part of his life.

Mike was impressed by the fact that I'd finished a postgraduate degree, and he liked the idea that I was writing a book. I hadn't begun writing it, though I too liked the idea of doing so, and was relieved when he didn't ask what it was about. Unlike Patrick, he wasn't interested in content. The suggestion that it existed was enough.

He introduced me to his friends, a mixed group of sculptors, actors, and hippies. They were all friendly, like him, and interesting. Despite not having a job or permanent home, he seemed to live very comfortably. His philosophy, he told me that first night, was simply 'Ask, and the universe will provide'.

We spent our time musing, eating at friends' houses, swimming, painting, or drawing, and gardening. The town was surrounded by small farms and large wineries, which meant you could cycle out to get cellar door specials and pick your own strawberries in ice-cream buckets. The days drifted by.

Our relationship was relaxed and companionable, rather than passionate. I wasn't in love, and didn't expect to be. Nevertheless, after a month or so, when his house-sitting spell finished, I suggested he move in with me. We already spent most of our time together, so it wasn't a big change for us.

My parents, on the other hand, weren't quite prepared for it.

They had been in Adelaide visiting family, and had decided to come down to see me, and meet Mike. As soon as they arrived, hot and flustered after an hour and a half in the car, he offered them a cup of tea. And then he took them on a tour of the small house. As they owned it, this initially seemed an odd thing to do but his point quickly became clear. He wanted to show them that we had pulled the two single beds together; he wanted to show them our sleeping arrangements.

I was only slightly less embarrassed by this behaviour than my parents, who left soon afterwards.

As soon as we'd waved them goodbye, I turned on him. 'What was that all about?'

He was calm, even patronising. 'I wanted to show them that you weren't their child anymore. That you're an adult and have an adult relationship. I thought if they understood that, they might stop trying to interfere with your life.'

My mother still called regularly and asked about my weight, my skin, and what I was actually doing. But was that interfering? I wasn't so sure. Wasn't it just parental concern? Sure, I hated it – particularly as her questions focused on things that also worried me – but I didn't think she was wrong to ask. I didn't feel that my parents needed to be taught a lesson. And certainly not by Mike.

'If I'm so grown up, then surely I should be dealing with my relationship with my parents – not you.' The incident made me not only angry but uneasy.

He sensed this. 'I was just trying to help. I don't like seeing you unhappy, and every time you put down the phone you are.' He looked hurt.

I forgave him: he was only doing it because he cared.

The beach lifestyle meant I was relaxed and much happier than I'd been for a long time, but I was also bored. The writing wasn't going well. I hadn't got beyond chapter two in fact, and had to admit that it wasn't bestseller material. Most bestsellers have more than ten double-spaced pages.

The solution seemed simple. I'd move to Melbourne and get a job. I didn't want to go back to Adelaide, and I wasn't ready for Sydney. When I went back there, I wanted to have achieved something positive. So far, all I'd managed to do was put on a stone, develop acne and bleach my hair blonde. So I chose Melbourne.

After eight hours on an interstate bus, I was in the city centre. It was cold, grey and very exciting. My older brother Archie and his fiancée let me stay with them, and, after two days of window-shopping, coffee sampling and half-hearted house hunting, I found a neat one-bedroom flat in Prahan.

I rang Mike and told him how it was clean and light and cheap. It was in a great area and, something I couldn't ignore, it was on Victoria Street. He had to come over and see it.

Chapter Thirteen

Mike didn't want to hear about Melbourne. He'd been visiting Katie, an ex-girlfriend, and had seen a 'for lease' sign in front of the house opposite hers. The house had a fabulous view of the sea, a big garden and was made of local sandstone. 'I've found a wonderful place here.'

He paused, expecting me to say something. 'Wouldn't it be fun to move in? To have our own house? Our own garden where we could grow things? Just imaginewe could sit on the verandah and watch the sunset. We could invite people over. There'd be no more house-sitting, group living or poky flats. Wouldn't it be fun?' And then came the crunch. 'But I can't do it without you.'

It didn't occur to me that this meant he literally couldn't do it without me. Instead, I was flattered: Mike wanted me to live with him in a real house. He didn't want me to move and to leave him.

'It sounds lovely.' I tried to sound enthusiastic as visions of my new life in Melbourne slipped away.

He hadn't lied. The place was charming and it had marvellous views. Together, we could afford it. I had my yellow sofas and the rest of my furniture brought down from Sydney and Mike retrieved his bits and pieces from his mother's house, where they'd been stored for some time. We then focused on getting the house and garden into order. It had been badly neglected for years, so there were plenty of things to do. Plenty to keep us occupied.

Mandy, Mike's daughter, came to visit regularly while we were painting rooms and planting vegetables. She loved the constant projects. Or it might have been that the projects always involved getting dirty.

One day, when we were digging in the garden, and Mike was out, she told me that she was really happy that her father had his own house again. Her stepfather, apparently, still called Mike a 'good-for-nothing-bum' but Mandy didn't believe it. He was doing well, wasn't he?

I was glad she didn't expect an answer.

Mike had spent the last ten years looking for both love and meaning in his life. He'd had a number of relationships since his marriage broke up, and a range of jobs. He'd tried church, therapy, crystals and self-improvement courses. He'd learnt the guitar and played cricket with the local club. My first impression of him had been of someone who didn't care what others thought, and was content to drift. However, after we moved in together it soon became evident that this attitude was a front. And increasingly, it was clear that he was only able to sustain it by using alcohol or dope.

What he really wanted was a stable job, a steady income and a glamorous woman. 'You'd look really good if you only lost a little weight,' he'd say to me, 'and if your skin were better. Why don't you wear skirts more? And high heels? Dress up a bit?'

His suggestions about clothes were just ridiculous. We lived at the beach. I didn't have a job. I didn't need to dress up. And I wasn't going to do so for him. His other criticisms were harder to deal with.

The truth was I'd now managed to put on nearly two stone since leaving Sydney, and the cystic acne now covered the tops of my thighs, my back and my shoulders. I wasn't looking my best. Part of me hated him for drawing attention to this but part of me responded to it – after all, it was the kind of honesty I had grown up with. My mother had a phrase for it: constructive criticism.

The acne disturbed me so much that I actually visited the local doctor. His theory was that it was caused by the Lithium, and that Lithium was also responsible for the weight gain. He had prescribed medication for the acne. It hadn't worked.

Mike knew this, and suggested his own solution. 'Why don't you just stop taking all of those drugs?' He thought that besides affecting my looks, they were affecting my mind. Detrimentally. He went on. 'How do I know who you really are anyway when you're on all that psychiatric crap?' He paused. 'How can I love someone I don't know?'

I wanted Mike to love me. I wanted someone to.

He went on, knowing he had my attention, 'Are these drugs supposed to make you feel better? You don't seem very happy to me. You'd be better off without them, better off just being able to feel your emotions naturally, and then deal with them. Why don't you just stop taking them?'

I had known that he didn't believe in medications but hadn't realised that he felt so strongly about mine. I didn't agree with him but I hated not fitting into my clothes, the constant tiredness and that it hurt to roll over in bed or even wear a bra. The spots didn't just look bad – it was painful.

If I stopped taking the pills, perhaps it would go away. Perhaps the weight would fall off; perhaps I'd be happy. I certainly wasn't now, not anymore. What did I have to lose?

The next morning I skipped my usual dose of Prozac, Lithium and the anti-acne drug and threw out the Largactil, which I occasionally took when I felt over-whelmed. It always knocked me out, and it wasn't until years later that I discovered that like Stelazine, it too was an anti-psychotic, not just a tranquillizer. I didn't take anything that evening. And I didn't take anything the following day. I'd been a bit worried that I'd sud-denly feel miserable, or that I might even want to hurt myself. But it seemed Mike was right, it was easy to get off them.

By the evening of the second day, however, I began to feel odd. At first I couldn't put my finger on it.

Every morning since we'd moved in, Mike would get up, walk out to the verandah and declare, gestur-ing towards the white cliffs, that we lived in Paradise. In the beginning, I had agreed. The place was unques-tionably beautiful. Now despite the cloudless skies and crystal-clear ocean, I began to answer him internally with, 'No, you dickhead, this is hell'. When he talked about what he wanted to do, the screenplays he wanted to write, the movies he wanted to direct, I was just annoyed. His prattle had at first been endearing, but was now excruciating.

At first it was just his words that upset me, and then it was the sound of his favourite chair scraping on the concrete. It went straight through my head, like fingernails on a blackboard. He didn't believe me when I told him.

Nor did he believe me when I said that I couldn't bear the sound of his voice, that he wasn't to talk to me. It was only when I started to cover my ears when he entered the room that he began to look worried.

If I went into the kitchen, I could not only see but could smell the acrid trail of ants leading to the cupboards. When I picked up the newspaper, I'd shudder involuntarily at the sensation of the paper in my hands. Soon, even walking across the bedroom floor barefoot became impossible as the soles of my feet screamed against the nylon in the carpet.

It wasn't long before I couldn't cope with the sensory overload and the only safe place was my bed. And I didn't want to cope. There was no point. I wasn't interested in eating, reading, showering or even moving, and instead spent my days dozing, or staring at the walls.

Katie, our neighbour, who was a nurse, came to visit after I'd been like this for nearly a week. She was furious with Mike. 'I can't believe that you suggested she go off those pills without medical supervision – they're not bloody vitamins.'

But Mike wasn't going to take any responsibility. 'She wanted to go off them, I didn't force her.'

Katie didn't believe him. She'd known him long enough to be familiar with his views on a lot of things, including medications. 'You know that she's sick? You know that she's not at all happy?'

'I don't know anything.' He sounded exasperated. 'She won't talk to me. She doesn't like the sound of my voice.'

'And what you've got to say, no doubt.' Katie then came back into my room – and it was mine, as Mike was now sleeping in the spare bedroom – and told me that she was going to call my psychiatrist. Mike would drive me up to town.

And that was that.

An appointment was organised for that afternoon. My bag was packed and the car filled with petrol. For the first time in days I got out of bed – clenching my teeth so as to be able to bear it – and showered and dressed.

As Mike and I drove to town I stared out the window. I didn't have enough energy to hurt myself but Katie was right, I wasn't in a good frame of mind and I didn't know what to do about it. I needed professional help.

When we arrived at the doctor's, Mike suggested that he join me in the appointment. That way we could talk about things together. He could help. The psychiatrist, Dr C, refused; he wanted to see me alone. Mike could sit in the waiting room, and wait.

An hour later, he drove me to the private psychiatric hospital I'd just been booked into. Dr C hadn't seen me for months but the change must have been significant. All I wanted, I said, was to go somewhere clean, cool, dark and quiet. Mike helped me in with my bags and was then asked to leave by the staff.

The relief was enormous. It really hadn't occurred to me how desperately unhappy I was until then. It wasn't just the side effects. It was Mike. And my life. I had been 'settling' for a life that I didn't really want and I knew that this was a mistake. 'Settling' was akin to giving up, or giving in, and I wasn't interested in either of these things but I was very, very tired.

The clinic was much the same as the psychiatric hospital I'd been in before. This time, however, instead of being in a ward, I was given my own room, my own bathroom, and had my meals delivered.

It was wonderful.

Later that evening Dr C dropped in to see how I was. He was obviously pleased that I'd agreed to go to hospital, and pleased to see me looking more comfortable. Initially, he suggested that I go back on to the Prozac and Lithium but I refused. I explained that it wasn't Mike's influence, but the other factors.

It took several days before we agreed that I did need to take something and what that 'something' might be. For the first time I felt as though I wasn't being patronised. I was being consulted. I agreed to start on another mood stabiliser, Tegretol. And he referred me to a dermatologist for my skin. There were drugs around that could fix it.

When I was able to get up, the first thing I did was head downstairs for a cigarette. After the third visit, I started to talk to the other smokers, and began to feel a bit more like myself. I then called two people – my aunt to let her know where I was, and an old childhood friend, Josh.

My aunt was obviously uncomfortable about the situation, in the same way my parents always were. I told her very little but the fact I was in a psychiatric hospital was enough. She suggested that we keep it quiet, and particularly that we shouldn't tell either of my grandmothers, who both lived close by. After all, I was supposed to be better, all of 'this kind of thing' was supposed to have been left behind.

Josh reacted in a very different way when I told him where I was. He was a builder and football player, and I'd not been sure about what he'd say but I wanted to speak to someone. Someone without an agenda. It was odd, we'd spent most of our childhoods together, and then when we'd left the property that was it. I hadn't seen him for fifteen years, until I arrived in Adelaide. Despite the gap, it was as if we'd only seen each other the previous week. His girlfriend had been incredibly jealous of this connection, which had made us laugh but her angry. As a result, I had seen nothing of him since moving to the beach.

He turned up an hour later, looking impossibly healthy and cheerful. 'So what on earth are you doing here, darl?'

I told him everything, all the things I hadn't told him when we'd last met. Then I'd focused on the good bits. When I'd finished, he shook his head. He was surprised that he hadn't heard about it on the grapevine, as our mothers were still friends. I had to explain then that it wasn't something anyone in my family talked about – to each other or to anyone else.

He was still amazed. 'I don't know what to say, or what I should do.'

Nothing, I didn't want him to do anything, and that was the point. I just wanted him to know.

As I began to feel better, I realised that I had to leave Mike, and the beach. There was no choice. The relationship wasn't making me happy and neither was the lifestyle. I needed to be doing something. I needed to be busy.

I'd already forbidden Mike to visit or call me, yet he was still surprised when I said I'd be moving out.

First, though, I needed a bit of time to recuperate. So when I left hospital, I went to stay with my maternal grandmother. For two more weeks, I did very little except sleep in, stroll round the block, eat light meals, and go to bed early. My grandmother didn't ask what had happened. Like everyone else in the family, she didn't believe in prying or discussing anything that might be unpleasant. But she encouraged me to use her phone to call my friends in Sydney.

Emily was delighted to hear from me, and to hear I hadn't gone back to the beach. She'd rung the beach house and had spoken to Mike, who'd lectured her on the evils of medication. He'd told her I was in hospital but that it didn't matter. I'd got off the stuff. I'd soon be myself again and he'd be living with a real person.

Emily was astonished, and immediately sat down to write to me. The letter eventually turned up at my grandmother's, and in it she said how worried she was about my relationship with Mike. Since I'd been with him, I'd hardly spoken to anyone outside his group of friends, and it wasn't good for me. He wasn't good for me. He was clearly mad. She hated to have to be so blunt but had to say it.

Peter offered to buy me an air ticket back to Sydney, so I could get a bit of perspective. Would I at least think about it?

By the end of the month, I had done a lot of thinking, and had a plan.

Josh drove me down to the beach to pack my things and pick up my clothes. I'd been wearing the same things for weeks but had hardly noticed. I told him that I didn't want to be left alone with Mike.

'I just want to speak to Vic in private, inside. There are things to say that, quite frankly, are none of your business. Don't treat me like an abusive husband.' Mike was shouting.

Josh was calm, and adamant, and told him again that we were just picking up my stuff. And that I didn't want to speak to him alone. It was pretty simple really.

Mike then turned to me again. 'What's wrong with you?'

What had I ever seen in him? 'There's nothing wrong with me. I just don't think we have anything to discuss. You've said often enough that you weren't in love with me, that I wasn't the kind of person you wanted, that I wasn't attractive. I'm doing you a favour by leaving. Don't pretend I'm not.'

Mike was insistent, and I suddenly realised it wasn't about me. 'You're treating me as if I've done something wrong. I haven't. I haven't done anything wrong. I've been honest – and is that so bad?' He was almost pleading now.

Josh and I walked past him with suitcases. Things had been thrown in, not packed. My furniture, which I loved, now felt tainted. The yellow sofas were marked and I couldn't even think about the bed. It could all stay. Mike said he'd buy it. When he could afford to.

Before I could finally leave, I had to say goodbye to Mandy. I liked her, and we'd got on well. She promised to write, to keep in touch, but I knew I'd be replaced. Mike would find another girlfriend soon enough – from what I heard, he always did.

Wanting never to have anything more to do with him, I left.

Chapter Fourteen

Two months later Mike was found washed up on a beach on the other side of the country, naked, bruised and dead.

During those two months, my life had changed enormously. I was barely recognisable as the girl he'd lived with.

My time at my grandmother's meant that I had all but given up cigarettes and had totally given up alcohol, which I'd been drinking a lot with Mike. I felt much better for it. Regular, balanced meals had also made a difference: I had energy. For years I'd alternated between starving myself and binging, to the extent that I'd forgotten what it was like just to eat because I was hungry. Now that I knew, I didn't want to lose this again. I had no doubt that these factors, as much as the change in medication and the move, were responsible for the way I felt. And I felt great.

I'd finally moved to Melbourne-a few months later than I'd intended, but I was there. My older brother, Archie, with whom I'd stayed the last time, let me sleep on the sofa bed of his front room while I set about finding somewhere to live.

Once I'd found that, the idea was to find a job.

After three days, during which I'd scoured the papers and visited a number of places, I began to feel that finding somewhere might be harder than I'd imagined. Sharing was certainly the most sensible option but I'd not seen anywhere that I really liked – and I wanted to like where I lived. But I needed to find somewhere soon, as it had become obvious that my brother's fiancée didn't want me staying any longer than was absolutely necessary. Archie himself was rarely home.

The problem might have been that I didn't fit into her lifestyle, which was about designer labels, gallery openings and film premieres, or it might have been that she was worried that I'd ask for support of some kind, either moral or financial. She knew about my history, and while chatty enough when we'd met for lunch in the past, and actually friendly when I'd attended their engagement party, the idea of me potentially disrupting her life must have really worried her.

So I accepted the offer of a corner of someone's sitting room. It was partitioned off, and had space for a bed, table and clothes rack. I'd lived once before in a room with particle board walls that didn't quite touch the ceiling so I could manage that. It was in a renovated three-storey former industrial building, so the spaces were large, and the kitchen and bathroom clean and modern. Sam, the owner, had some nice pieces of furniture, and there were flowers on the table. Surely someone who bothered to put flowers on the table couldn't be too bad? He was a barrister and, I soon discovered, out a lot. He told me that he normally rented the space – now my space – to backpackers, which made sense. Other people might have insisted on a door. He also told me where I could find a job as a barmaid.

He directed me to the old pub diagonally opposite his building – so less than two minutes' walk away. I had to speak to the boss, a tough and terrifying woman, and tell her that I was staying with him. She frowned slightly, and then, when I said I had no experience, allowed me a trial night. I could pick up glasses, and she'd see how I went. I was to report for work at 6 pm in a white shirt and black pants. Pants mind you, not jeans.

I spent the evening being yelled at, hassled, pushed and finally, I was employed. She'd let me know later which shifts I was to do.

I had both a room and a job. Things were looking up.

After several weeks of working in the bar at night, where I had finally been promoted to pouring drinks, and at a nearby café during the day, I was contacted by the Commonwealth Employment Agency, or the CES as it was then known. As I'd been on their books continuously for over six months, I was officially one of the 'long-term unemployed'. In reality I'd been on their books for much longer, but not continuously, as sickness benefits apparently didn't count.

As one of the 'long-term unemployed' I was to have a case manager, training, and would be put in a subsidised job for six months. It was bizarre: I didn't think of myself as unemployable anymore and I wasn't. I had two jobs – not that they knew this.

My case manager shook her head as she looked through her files. It was going to be difficult, apparently. 'There's something going at a magazine. They need an administrative assistant. The job's not available for a month but it might suit you. Can you type?'

I had to tell the truth. 'No.'

She sighed. Then she grimaced. 'They really want someone who can type. They've specified that it's essential on the form. But how about you go along for the interview anyway, it would be good practice.' She paused. 'I know you've got two degrees, but it would be better not to sound too ambitious. They only want an assistant. Nothing more.' She repeated this about four times in the space of an hour, then told me that I had to enrol in a course to improve my employability. What about computing? I had no choice but to agree: if I didn't they'd cut off my allowance.

When I turned up at the CES training centre the following Monday, I was asked to do a spelling and comprehension test. I explained that I had a Master's degree in English Literature, so really didn't need to do the test. By this time my work had been marked and, surprisingly given the circumstances, had been passed. I'd been awarded my degree in absentia. The girl behind the rather grubby beige desk looked at me blandly and shrugged. 'Doesn't matter. You still have to do this.'

I then spent four hours each weekday morning for the next month learning how to design restaurant menus and invitations to parties.

During the first week, I heard from the CES. The people at the magazine wanted to see me.

When I was getting ready for the interview, I realised that for the first time since I'd hit puberty, I had really clear skin and fine, fine pores. The dermatologist I'd been to see while in the clinic had prescribed Roaccutane and I'd been on it for six weeks. The difference was incredible, the acne had cleared up entirely on my back, and though my face hadn't ever been affected, it now looked amazing. And I wasn't suffering from any of the side effects that I'd been warned about, like split lips, a painfully dry nose, dandruff. On the contrary, I looked radiant. My hair had been dyed back to close to its natural colour, and, since there was so little oil in it, it too looked soft rather than lank.

I owned only one jacket, and one pair of winter pants, so dressing for the interview was easy. As I perched on a chair in the bathroom, trying to see myself in the mirror, I realised that I really wanted this job. The CES officer's voice came back to me. 'Don't show that you are ambitious. This is just admin.' I could do that.

The interview was in the main office, which had overflowing bookshelves, large windows and a tatty old Persian carpet on the floor. I sat in front of a large table, facing the editor, the editorial assistant and the director of the company which owned the magazine.

They'd all read my resumé but it quickly became apparent that they weren't interested in talking about it – except for the editor, Eva, who wanted to know what a gatekeeper was. I explained that it involved sitting in a booth, reading a book, and letting cars in and out. It was one of the many part-time jobs I'd had at uni.

They had been about to give up on the CES program, as the last few people they'd interviewed were painfully unsuitable. It was almost as though the CES was just sending people over in order for them to brush up on their interview skills. The previous applicant was a contract fencer by trade, and a handyman. The director, Tim, had been pushing to hire him, as he liked the idea of having someone around to fix up shelves and replace light fittings.

After half an hour or so, Tim, and Jill, the editorial assistant, left the room and Eva offered me the job. Shocked, I immediately accepted but – aware that they'd find out sooner or later – felt compelled to confess two things. First, that I couldn't touch-type and second, that I'd recently come out of a mental institution.

Chapter Fifteen

The CES officer had been right, there was a lot of typing to do but I'd spent the couple of weeks between being offered the job and starting it, learning to type properly, so I didn't mind at all. In fact I loved it. And I loved making the coffee, and doing all the other mundane admin jobs. It didn't matter that it wasn't particularly challenging. It was fun, and everyone was nice to me.

In my spare time – I was only working four days a week so I had quite a bit – I decided to try writing an article. Not for my employer's magazine, but for another, or for a newspaper. I wanted to write about mental illness; not about my own experience, but about other people's. I had heard there was a collection of in-patients' art at one of the public psychiatric hospitals. It was the product of many years, and many art therapy classes. (How I would have loved art therapy: none of the hospitals I went to ever offered it. One clinic had a punching bag, but it wasn't the same.) When I rang the curator and said I wanted to write about the collection, it was surprisingly easy to organise a tour of the whole institution.

The hospital was the kind of cold, daunting and forbidding place I'd envisaged when – several years ago now – it had first been suggested that I needed some 'time out'. Unlike private hospitals, which were like health clubs with security, this place resembled a prison. The paint was peeling and the furniture in the reception area was practical and scuffed. Linoleum floors meant that sounds carried.

One of the male nurses took me around. As he talked, I thought to myself that this journalism thing was pretty straightforward really. You just had to come up with an idea, speak to few people, ask a few questions and remember to listen to them when they answered. I could do that.

In the common room, patients sat around watching television, pacing and staring out of the window at the leafless trees. That was the only similarity to the hospitals I'd been in. The bedrooms, if you could call them that, were spartan. I had been lucky to be able to go somewhere else, somewhere that cost five hundred dollars a day for the uninsured.

When I was shown the modern-day equivalent of the padded cell, I was staggered. Somehow I'd doubted that they existed. These ones had an open loo in one corner and a tiny window high in the wall. Painted a familiar, supposedly soothing, shade of pale pink, they looked like places for housing criminals, not sick people. But as the nurses asked, what other options were there? If someone was violent, psychotic and dangerous, they had to be locked up – for their own good, as much as for everyone else's.

Resources were limited and it was obvious that it wasn't just the patients who were unhappy. But things weren't going to change: the government didn't actually want people in the hospitals, so why increase funding?

The collection of psychiatric art was housed in a building across the park. The artworks were grouped into sections according to the category of diagnosis, with each artwork accompanied by a small note about the patient who produced it. The differences between sections were immediately apparent. Generally, the images from the depressive group were dark, still and claustrophobic. They managed to convey a sense of isolation, frustration or plain despair. Conversely, the few paintings by those suffering from mania were vibrant, expansive and exhausting. The works painted, or made – as there was also embroidery and sculpture – by people suffering from forms of schizophrenia often showed an acute attention to tiny, tiny detail. The notes were enlightening. These complex works, they said, reflected the perspectives of people who were trying to control their worlds through art.

The commentary also illustrated the importance of the collection: while offering relief for the patients, it also provided valuable insights into their minds. Given that so many forms of mental illness were so difficult to articulate, I could see why most of the visitors were students studying psychology or medicine.

I thought the collection should be open to the general public.

At home in my corner room, I started writing. As the place was unheated, I sat at my computer wearing a hat and scarf. If I'd been able to type in them, I also would have worn my gloves. Five hours later, I'd written something about the hospital, the art and the founder of the collection. I didn't know if it was any good but I did think it was interesting – and, maybe, important. If people could just understand how it actually felt to be depressed, obsessed, frightened, out of control, maybe they'd be more tolerant. More understanding.

Already, as I began to believe that I could have a career, could fit in, I'd started to want to hide my past. I wanted to be like everyone else.

At work on Monday, Eva spotted me trying, discreetly, to photocopy my article. She knew about my history so I had nothing to lose. I let her read it.

As she sat at her desk, I tried to keep busy, and to pretend I didn't care, it didn't matter. Nevertheless, it was hard to forget that I'd given my work to one of the country's most outspoken critics: what if she hated it? What if she told me I couldn't write?

Ten minutes later, she congratulated me. She liked it. It wasn't right for the magazine of course, but she liked it. Did I want to do something for her? Was I interested in book reviewing?

Was I? I couldn't think of anything better. Eva was actually offering me money to read a book! She also suggested that I contact a friend of hers who edited another magazine, an art magazine, and send him the piece I'd written. He turned it down, but kindly. If I wanted to do something else, he said, I should call him. We could talk about it.

But by then I'd decided that I'd concentrate on reviewing. I put the piece away.

Chapter Sixteen

Things were going well. I was fit, I was happy and I was busy. All I needed now was a real place to live. As soon as I finished my review I'd start looking.

It only occurred to me as I was trying to write my first sentence that the last time I'd written a book review was at school. Perhaps inspiration would come if I left it for a bit. If I cleaned, ironed, dusted. The place was spotless and I had finally sat down at my computer when the phone rang.

It was my aunt from Adelaide. I was surprised to hear from her and chatted for a bit about nothing in particular. Then came the truth. She'd just finished reading the local paper. They'd found Mike's body on a Sydney beach. According to the article, it had taken several days to identify him, as he hadn't been reported missing, and there were no documents nearby. There would be an inquest but at this stage it looked like he'd jumped from a cliff. There were no suspicious circumstances.

I didn't know what to say. I didn't want to cry and I didn't feel angry. I felt nothing. Blank. She gave me the time and date of the funeral, which was to be held in Adelaide.

Since I'd left, Mike and I had barely spoken. His voice had still irritated me. He owed me money and, although he had recently inherited quite a lot, he didn't want to pay his debt to me. He kept fobbing me off, telling me the cheque was in the mail, and it was a line I was sick of hearing. It hadn't even been funny the first time.

I knew he'd moved to Sydney, with a young woman he'd met while she was waitressing at a party he'd thrown. As they were passing through Melbourne on the way there, he actually rang me and suggested that I meet them both at the train station. I'd like her, he said. She was like me. He couldn't understand why I didn't want to see him – or her.

It was to be our last conversation.

It wasn't until I spoke to friends at his wake that we began to put together a picture of his final weeks. He'd spent nearly $30,000 in less than three months and died virtually broke. No-one could work out where the money had gone at first, until his brother – who, Mike had told me many times, had never liked me – asked if I knew about his gambling. I didn't. Autoteller receipts had been found on the floor of his rented room in Sydney showing large, daily withdrawals. He'd spent it on poker machines; $30,000 on poker machines, dope and alcohol.

He had also left a diary and the entry on what was probably the day he died was rambling and barely coherent, though it was clear he planned to kill himself. Also in the room were books on self-healing and New Age spirituality. His last phone call had been to a woman he'd done group therapy with some years before.

On his last weekend, he had flown back to Adelaide and visited everyone he cared about, telling them how well things were working out. He saw almost forty people in two days, it turned out. He had left his dog with a friend, promising to collect it later. My grandmother, who was then 90, asked him to leave when he arrived on her doorstep at 8 am on the Saturday. She didn't tell me this until after he died. She hadn't thought it important.

The overnight train trip home after the funeral was miserable. The heating didn't work, the rain leaked through the side window, dampening my blanket, and there was no food available. I had twelve hours to stare out into the blackness and think.

Why didn't I feel more? Why was I still angry, not with his decision, but with him? Maybe it was pride. Maybe it was because he had been happy to live with me, sleep with me, criticise me and let me look after his daughter but he hadn't been in love with me. When things had been going well, when we'd been having fun, he'd said carefully, 'I love you but I'm not in love with you. I'll never be in love with you.' I didn't love him, but that wasn't the point. Just because it hadn't broken my heart didn't mean it didn't hurt, or that I didn't resent him for it.

The train drew into a cold, wet morning and as I trudged up from the station, I was looking forward to having a long hot shower and crawling into bed. Only I couldn't: there were two strangers asleep under my doona.

Stunned, I stopped only long enough to clean my teeth and wash my face before heading out to find a newspaper and a café. As I looked through the various share accommodation ads for smokers, non-smokers, females, cat lovers and professionals, one ad in particular caught my attention. 'Small room in city warehouse, very central, suitable for travellers.' At the bottom was my housemate's mobile number. Sam knew I'd been thinking about leaving, and must have been planning to show my room to people while I was away. I hadn't told him I was only going for two days.

I was determined not to go home until I'd found somewhere new.

By the third dark, grungy, dirty house I was ready to cry. Wasn't there anywhere in the whole of Melbourne that I could both afford and like? By the time I reached the final place on my list I was sure there wasn't but I tried to be friendly to the two girls who lived there. At the beginning of the day I'd been cautious about talking too much about myself, and didn't want to complain about my current flatmate, as people might think it was my fault – or that I was difficult. But it was 5 pm, I was exhausted and didn't care anymore. I told the girls about the funeral, the couple in my bed and the ad. I admitted that I hadn't slept or washed since leaving Adelaide. After half an hour of swapping stories about flatmates from hell, I got up to leave. They had a few more people to see that afternoon but said they'd call me. Even if they didn't, I felt better for talking about it all.

As I was crossing the park nearby, I heard someone calling what sounded like my name. Knowing few people in town, I ignored it. And then I was tapped on the shoulder.

Did I want to move in? And how soon could I do so?

Chapter Seventeen

The house was a terrace, built in around 1880, and renovated badly in the early 1970s. The walls were scuffed, the paint peeling and, in the bedrooms, the carpet was stained. It was also five minutes from cinemas, supermarkets and cafés, and a ten-minute walk to work. And it was warm.

To me, it was perfect.

I put everything I'd been through over the last few years – including Mike – out of my mind, and threw myself into my new life.

Work kept me busy, and in addition to coffee-making I took responsibility for advertising and marketing. It was a small operation after all. It wasn't that I was ambitious, more that I was happy. I wanted to learn as much as I could about how it all worked. I wanted to do well. Eva took seriously my suggestions about how things could be reorganised. She took me seriously. I wasn't just the work experience girl on contract for six months: I was someone who had opinions, someone worth listening to. Whatever I did, she praised.

At first, I held my breath, waiting for the outburst, the fury, the moment she discovered I wasn't perfect. But it didn't ever happen – and the phrase 'constructive criticism' wasn't in her vocabulary.

But as the days went by, I became increasingly nervous about something else: what would happen at the end of six months? The magazine clearly couldn't afford to take me on without the government grant and I was terrified of being unemployed again. I'd discovered what it was like to get up in the morning and want to go to work. And I didn't want to be like Mike. I didn't want to reach my mid-forties without a vocation. I didn't want to be lost, or searching. So I put in an application to do a diploma of education. At least then I'd have something, as they say, 'to fall back on'. The idea of standing up in front of a class wasn't the least bit appealing but I didn't know what else I could do.

But it wasn't just the job that I was enjoying. It was more than that.

People had begun to respond to me in a different way. I wasn't someone to be wary of, or nervous about. My housemates must have noticed my scars but didn't ever comment. Instead they seemed to take me at face value. Or rather, perhaps, at my own value. I didn't feel ashamed of myself any longer, or think that I was a failure. In fact, I didn't really even think about how I felt at all, which was a big change. I went to work, to the movies, cooked dinner, gossiped. Life, for once, was about what was going on outside my head, not inside.

Then the editorial assistant resigned and Eva offered me her job. Finally now, when my parents' friends asked sensitively, 'So how is Victoria?' they could reply that I was very well. That I'd got through my difficult period, my difficult phase. Everything now was back on track: I just need to find a nice man.

And that was where Christian came in. He was exactly what my parents had in mind. A good-looking, clean-cut, well-spoken corporate lawyer, he was introduced to me by a friend at a ball. I'd turned up in a dinner suit, rather than a strapless dress, as I had too many memories of university balls to want to appear as something I wasn't. If someone was to be interested in me, then it was not going to be for what I was wearing.

As I arrived I didn't think anyone would be interested: there were a lot of very beautiful women around, in very beautiful, very expensive dresses. But I did feel very comfortable, and oddly relaxed. I didn't know these people – only Lilly, the friend who had organised the table – so what did it matter?

Christian was on my left-hand side and even as I sat down I decided I didn't like him. He had the look of a man who is very, very pleased with himself. He was too attractive, too smooth. His teeth were too white. The only way to deal with him was not to take him seriously. So I teased him mercilessly all evening. I wasn't interested in him, after all. It didn't matter how I treated him.

I had a great night, and went home alone.

The following week, our table met again. We'd won the door prize, a free meal at a local Thai restaurant. I arrived early and Christian sat next to me. I was delighted – it was another opportunity to bait someone who so obviously deserved it. He flirted shame-lessly, but it wasn't serious. How could it be?

He was funny and clever, as well as good-looking and successful. We were not in the same league.

On Monday night Lilly called. Christian wanted to see me but wasn't sure whether I was available, or even interested. I'd confused him apparently, and he wasn't used to that.

The date started badly, with rain and a film adap-tion of a Thomas Hardy novel. It was depressing and distressing, involving child suicide and poverty. Things did improve over dinner – at another Thai restaurant we'd agreed on after discovering we'd both spent time in Thailand. He'd gone with a girlfriend, and I'd gone for a holiday between degrees. We bond-ed by swapping horror stories of stomach upsets. By the end of the evening I'd decided that he was human after all.

Soon we started seeing each other a few times a week, and doing very normal couple-like things: going to restaurants, pubs, galleries, bands and watching videos. The only thing we didn't do was sleep togeth-er, which suited me fine. It was refreshing to find a bloke who liked me, was happy to be seen with me, and liked doing things that involved actually leaving the house.

One crisp Saturday morning, a little while after we'd first met, we drove up to the mountains for lunch, as he knew a restaurant up there he wanted to take me to. I was still amazed that he was interested in me, but pretended otherwise. I sensed that letting him see that I wasn't confident would put him off. So I pretended, and, when I was with him my past seemed a very, very long way away. I was a different person.

Christian was going to have to be told at some stage about at least a little of my history as I didn't want him seeing my scars and jumping to his own conclusions. It seemed like a good day to do it.

After lunch, as we strolled along a nearby path in the bush, bonding over the discovery that our parents had used riding crops on us both as children, I casually asked him if he knew anything about mental illness. Nothing much, he said. Ignoring this, I dived in. I kept to the most digestible bits, the depression and the hospitals. I skipped quickly over the cutting.

'I'm fine now though,' I said. 'Things are great.' And I told him about Tegretol, the mood stabiliser. It felt much better now that it was out in the open. Not telling him had been difficult, a burden. I had felt as though I were hiding something. I had been hiding something.

It took a few minutes before he said anything. Why wasn't he talking? The alternatives flashed through my head. Would he pity me? Would he, like Mike, suggest other ways that I could heal myself? Would he, like one of the many men I'd slept with, kiss my scars, say they were just a part of me, and then vanish the next morning, never to call again? Or would he, like Patrick, just accept it and move on to another subject?

The day I'd first cut myself a switch in my head had been flicked. Instead of feeling horror, I felt nothing, and although I no longer wanted to hurt myself, my episodes of self-harm still felt normal for me in a way. I'd sometimes forget it still shocked other people.

Christian was from a very stable, balanced family. He had three brothers, had gone to a private school, and was now a solicitor. He'd worked hard at university and still kept up with his various ex-girlfriends. He told me he'd never met anyone with a mental illness before. Or – he corrected himself – no-one that admitted it.

He then looked away from me. Since we were being honest, I should know that he already had a girlfriend. Only she was in Spain for six months. He wasn't sure how he'd feel when she got back but spending time with me had made him realise that he still really cared about her. What he was looking for was a fling, someone to have a bit of fun with. Given my situation, I wasn't the right person. He didn't want to do that to me. I was a nice girl. He cared about me.

I couldn't believe it. It wasn't me he cared about. It was himself. He didn't want things to get messy and complicated. I wasn't the easygoing person he'd assumed I was: I was a potential risk.

There was an arrogance – and pragmatism, if I was honest – about Christian's attitude that I hadn't been prepared for. Questions, yes, surprise yes, but rejection, no. I hadn't calculated on that.

Several days later, I called him and he relented. We had dinner and then, for the first time, slept together. The following morning he flew to Sydney for a meeting.

He didn't call and he didn't call.

At the end of the week, I picked up the phone.

It had been a mistake he said, he was sorry. He then remembered to uninvite me to his New Year's Eve party, and it was over.

Chapter Eighteen

I threw myself into work, into writing reviews and into exercising. I just needed to keep busy, I told myself.

But it wasn't just the break-up with Christian that was bothering me. Eva's husband had died.

She was devastated. They'd been married for over twenty years and were devoted to each other.

People said that it would just take time. We all had to give her time. This didn't worry me, she could take as long as she needed to as far as I was concerned, and I was happy to pick up extra tasks. There was little else I could do – or that anyone else could do, for that matter.

As the months passed, it became apparent that Eva's grief wasn't abating, it was turning into something else. She had stopped eating, and was surviving, it seemed, on coffee. She was very thin and pale now, and had lost all her vitality. But work was all she had, and there was no question of her taking a break. She believed in what the magazine stood for, and it became the reason she got out of bed in the morning.

Eventually, she was unable to hide from her boss the fact she wasn't well. He took me aside: was she turning up every day? Was her work suffering? What could be done to help?

Nothing. There was nothing that could be done, I told him. She was unhappy, but it wasn't affecting her work. I promised to let him know if it did.

By letting me take care of the details, Eva was able to focus on commissioning. It was a situation that suited us both. I liked the extra responsibility, and could manage it, and she was able to do what she was best at – and what she liked doing. The main thing was to ensure that the magazine still came out on time once a month. She'd get through this period, and then things would be back to normal.

The day she came in with her hands in bandages wasn't particularly memorable. She said she'd had an accident at a barbeque on Sunday. We were all horrified, and sympathetic. The burns must have hurt enormously. It wasn't fair, to have that happen, on top of everything else.

The bandages eventually came off, revealing wounds not on her palms, or fingers, where you'd expect, but on the tops of her hands. It was odd but at the time I didn't think too much about it. They looked like they were healing well, and she'd seemed better recently. Eva was known for her dry wit and outspoken opinions, and it had been reassuring to see glimpses of her old, lively self. It had changed the entire mood of the office. Perhaps the grey cloud was at last lifting?

It wasn't until she came in the following week with a bandage back on that I realised what she was doing.

She said that they needed to be dressed again, but was evasive about why. I wasn't disturbed or disappointed, more than anything I was surprised. She was in her fifties after all. Wasn't self-harm something people did as teenagers? Or in their twenties? Wasn't it something people grew out of? I certainly hadn't had any desire to do anything like that since I'd been in Melbourne, and now thought of myself as cured. The depression I knew might come back, because that was how it worked, but I thought the urge to self-harm had gone for good.

I decided not to say anything to her, as it was her business, no-one else's. From my own experience, I knew that nothing anyone else said was going to help anyway. It became obvious, as the weeks turned into months, and the bandages came off and on, off and on, that she wasn't coping. And everyone knew it. Not just the staff and her boss, but also the contributors. It was only willpower keeping her going, with the aid of alcohol, cigarettes and a lunchtime cappuccino.

People – friends, writers, editors – began to ring up, asking about her health. Was she all right? She was very thin and they'd heard about her hands. What had happened to them? What did I know?

They just wanted to help.

I was her assistant, not her nurse, so always said she was perfectly well. If they had any questions about her health, they could ask her. There often seemed to be a scurrilous edge to these calls. If they'd asked outright if she was hurting herself, I might have given them a straight answer. But it seemed no-one could utter the words. They could mention depression, melancholy, grief, but not ask if she was hurting herself.

The reason I didn't talk about it with her was not that it was a taboo subject but because she didn't discuss it with me. She knew that I had scars on my arm; she could have asked but chose not to. While she leant heavily on me at work, she obviously didn't want me to take her problems home.

But I couldn't help it.

I liked – trusted – my housemates, and could have confided in them. I could have rung Emily or Peter. Or even Josh. The thing was, I felt that it was my secret as well, so I kept it at home and at work. Also, I didn't want to shatter the illusion that my life was going well. If I admitted that Eva was burning herself, it would draw attention to my own past. It was easier to say nothing. If someone asked about work I was always positive, upbeat. Things were great. Busy, but great. I loved it.

The trouble was, I still loved it but things weren't great. The combination of dealing with Eva's health and the general stress of putting together a magazine on a tight budget began to get to me. I noticed that I had a stomach-ache pretty much all the time. It was tense muscles, nothing more dramatic. Of course you're tense, I told myself, you're in a stressful situation. This is a normal reaction. What you need to do is manage things sensibly: exercise more, eat properly, get enough sleep. This is enough, I told myself. You can keep in control this way. Things will get better soon.

You just need to hold on.

After months of forcing myself to cope, I found that it wasn't becoming easier. The strain wasn't the work-load. What was really getting to me was Eva's prob-lem, and pretending it didn't exist. Pretending that she was fine. Pretending that it didn't affect me.

There was an Italian restaurant downstairs from the office. Each month, after the magazine had been put to bed, we'd all go there for a drink. The restau-rant staff knew us well, and our chardonnay, nuts and ashtray would arrive automatically. As Eva and I sat there one afternoon, after everyone else had headed off, it seemed a good time to give her some advice. I'd agonised before doing it, as I didn't want to say any-thing that would alter our relationship, but in the end I thought it would be wrong not to.

As casually as I could, I told her that self-harm was habit-forming. There, I'd said it. I didn't want to see her get caught in that cycle. If she knew of the mental dangers involved perhaps that would help stop her doing it. It had only been six months. Perhaps it was-n't too late?

'I know,' she said. 'This isn't the first time. I used to do it a long time ago, before I got married.' But she appreciated that I'd said something, and she appreciat-ed that I treated her normally at work. It did make things easier, she said.

And she was seeing someone about it. She also took something when things were bad, she said. A drug called Largactil: this was why she sometimes slurred her words. It said something about her stami-na; I couldn't even stay upright after taking a child size amount of this drug.

It worried me that the urge to hurt yourself didn't necessarily vanish, but might just lie dormant for years. Would I find myself in twenty years' time unwrapping razor blades again? It was an awful thought. Did it mean that I too would never really be cured?

The truth was – no matter how much I tried to hide it – I knew I wasn't even close to cured: the urge to cut myself had come back.

While I was at work I was safe. My mind was occupied with editing, advertising strategies, marketing plans, making lists of which articles weren't yet in, which ones I had to chase and what images we needed to use. There were phones and emails to answer, proofreaders to organise, and the post to go through.

Like Eva, increasingly I was finding work a place of refuge.

I used to enjoy the short solitary walk to the office in the mornings. The air was fresh, there was little traffic, and it was the perfect time to work out what I needed to do for the day. Now I could be ambushed at any point along the way by images of knives and razors and my own arms, seeping blood.

At home I began shutting out my flatmates and friends. I'd turn down invitations and I wasn't interested in chatting idly on the back steps with the rest of the household. It was as though withholding the information about what was happening at work meant I couldn't talk about anything at all.

Small things began to annoy me, and I became uncharacteristically short-tempered.

We'd all moved house en masse to a larger terrace nearby. Along with Rachael and Alison, who'd been in the previous place, we'd found two new tenants for the extra rooms. I became increasingly intolerant of both. One, I felt, watched too much television. He was Scottish, and perfectly pleasant, but had just this one hobby. The other, a musician, played his cello, and spoke too loudly. He just laughed when I asked him to keep the noise down. His room was next to mine, and I'd lie in bed at night gritting my teeth, hating him. The radio, which was always on in the kitchen in the mornings, began to bother me too. As the other four people in the household liked it, I couldn't turn it off.

I tried to tell myself I was being irrational. These things hadn't worried me before, and they didn't worry anyone else. As I became less interested in food, and more interested in sleeping, it became obvious that I wasn't well. I ignored the symptoms although I knew what they meant. What I couldn't ignore, but could at least try to hide, was a new, embarrassing habit. I developed a need to check that the doors were locked. Sometimes, I'd return to the house five or more times before finally being satisfied that the front door was closed. It meant getting ready at least half an hour earlier than I needed to.

Rather than seeing a doctor, or talking to someone, I decided to move. It had made me feel better before.

Chapter Nineteen

I convinced everyone that this latest move was about growing up. In my late twenties now, with a permanent job, it was time to have my own place. I wanted my own furniture, my own bathroom. I'd cook, I'd have dinner parties and people to stay. I sounded so convincing that I almost believed my own story.

It didn't take long for the views, the space and the privacy to lose their importance.

I had a nasty bout of the flu, and, nearly deaf with infections in both ears, visited the local doctor. His surgery was in the front room of his house, and the walls were covered in signed photographs of football players. This immediately made me doubt that he was the right person for me, but along with needing antibiotics, I knew that it was time to find myself a new psychiatrist. I'd not seen one since leaving Adelaide, and hated to admit that I needed to. But it was clear that I did.

I gave the doctor a three-minute summary of my past and let him know about my new symptoms. In the past two months since I'd been living alone, I'd become increasingly obsessive. It wasn't just door-checking anymore, or the urge to hurt myself. I'd stopped cooking, as I'd become paranoid about using the gas stove. Despite no evidence, I was sure it leaked. I'd also developed irrational fears about eating certain foods, including what had been staples, such as fish and chicken. It was difficult to work out what I could eat – what wouldn't, to be honest, poison me. I was managing on toast, coffee, vegetables and soup.

In my spare time, I'd often sit in a chair near the phone, trying to control my breathing. And wondering at what point I should pick up the receiver and tell someone what was happening. The trouble was, none of these things made sense: what would I say?

The doctor suggested that my breathing problem was stress-related, and that I'd be okay if I concentrated on something else. I should mention it to the psychiatrist though, like everything else. Had I ever had a panic attack?

Great, I thought. Another thing to add to the list. 'No,' I told him, 'I don't think so.'

By the time I showed up at the psychiatrist's office for my consultation a month later, it was taking all my energy just to get to work. A promotion meant that I was now assistant editor, and as far as everyone at the magazine knew, I was in great form. I appeared to be the same chirpy, efficient person that I'd always been. It was essential: Eva was now making suicide attempts on the weekends.

We couldn't both be seen to be losing it.

My friends later admitted that they knew something was wrong, but as I refused to admit it, there was nothing they could do. Besides, they saw very little of me. I stopped going out, didn't answer the phone, and my mail mounted up, unopened on top of the fridge.

My parents – my mother in particular – couldn't understand why I wasn't more upbeat. They were very proud of my progress at the magazine, subscribing to it and showing their friends my reviews. How could I tell them that something was wrong? They thought that after my last stint in hospital, and the change of medication, I'd been cured.

The new psychiatrist seemed pleasant enough initially, and I relaxed a little. I knew how this all worked. However, as I started talking, I noticed that he appeared to be nodding off. I stopped.

'Are you listening?' I asked.

'Mmm. Go on,' came the answer.

I tried to go on but found it difficult. Apparently what I had to say wasn't quite interesting enough to keep him awake. Was I just another neurotic woman to him? Just another person for whom he'd prescribe antidepressants and a weekly visit?

If that's what he thought, he was wrong on both counts: firstly, I'd developed a phobia about medications, and secondly, I wasn't going to see him again. I decided that I'd have to come up with my own solution. My biggest fear now was hospital. If I could just keep out of there, then I was alright. I didn't want to fall back into that pattern – or become the person that I had been.

Several years before, when I'd had very short hair, I'd been at a party. A bloke, a boyfriend of a friend, had come up to me. He'd asked if they'd had to cut off my hair when I was in hospital. For the shock treatment.

It was a joke apparently, not that I found it funny. When I'd first been admitted to the clinic, there'd been a doctor in there suffering from depression. She was lovely, friendly and sad. The next time I saw her was at a train station. She recognised me immediately but apologised: she couldn't remember who I was, just that she had a warm feeling toward me. The electro-convulsive therapy – shock treatment – had helped her depression, but temporarily screwed up her memory.

I didn't want to go back to that world.

On the tram on the way home I decided that the only possible solution was to resign and move back to Sydney, before something happened. Much as I hated to leave my job, the alternative was much more frightening.

My plan was to say to Eva that Melbourne was too cold, and that I was missing my friends. It was weak but I didn't want to tell the truth. I didn't want to hurt her and admit that the pressure was too much.

My parents were devastated. What on earth was I doing? Leaving a job, for no good reason, what kind of person does that? What kind of daughter had they raised? My father had been at a dinner party recently and had been told about Eva's 'problem'. This was sad of course, but they couldn't see how it affected me.

My mother told me that I was mad to leave the magazine. I didn't bother to say I'd go mad if I stayed. What was the point?

Eva was shocked when I handed in my resignation, but understood that there was no point arguing. If she knew why I was going, she didn't let on. Instead she wrote me a glowing reference. Eva's boss knew more, and mentioned the possibility of another job, if I wanted to stay in Melbourne.

I would have liked to accept it, but it was too late. I couldn't. I'd said I was leaving Melbourne so that's what I had to do. If I'd said I just wanted a change of scenery, a new job in the same city, Eva wouldn't have believed me. At least my chilblain-covered fingers were a testament to the fact that I really didn't like the cold.

Chapter Twenty

Once I was back in Sydney, my mother kept reminding me that it had been the scene of my first 'breakdown'. Wasn't it dangerous to be back there? There were government jobs where they were: perhaps I could come home?

There, I thought, was a retrograde step.

Her constant refrain didn't help my own confidence about my decision, but I had learnt that a 'breakdown' wasn't about location. I could have one – whatever that was – anywhere.

By this stage, Archie had left his fiancée and moved to Sydney. He'd fallen for someone else in Melbourne so while distracted was much happier. He also had a spare room.

We hadn't lived together since I was sixteen, when he left home. In those days he was moody, selfish and angry. When he wasn't playing sport, he and my mother fought. I just tried to keep out of it; it was easier that way. Told he'd never make anything of himself without a university education, he'd been determined to do well. And he had. But it had come at a price, with very high stress levels. It had taken him ten years to find a way to deal with them without cigarettes and alcohol, as so many others in his industry did. He had rediscovered sport.

And he'd discovered Melissa. Instead of cocktail parties and gallery openings, she liked barbeques and pubs; instead of designer clothes, she was happy in jeans. Her attitude had rubbed off on Archie.

We weren't close now, but he was happy for me to stay as long as I needed to.

Even after a week the urge to hurt myself faded, and the flashes of violence went through my mind only occasionally – and they seemed to appear out of habit more than anything else. As a result they were less threatening. Similarly, the desire to constantly check locks, which had intensified when I lived alone and had no-one to hide it from, now receded. To go back to check the front door two or three times was nothing. It wasn't like the period just before I left Melbourne, when I would have to go back eight or ten times, after each time, getting downstairs and thinking, did I imagine checking or did I do it? I'd then go upstairs, check again and get downstairs, only to have the same thought again.

Even my food phobias became less of an issue.

In all, I began to feel close to normal again.

Archie's flatmate, Carol, was friendly and outgoing. She was always keen for a coffee or a chat and it wasn't long before she asked about my arm. I was taken aback but I appreciated her directness and told her the truth. Well, not at first – at first I gave her the bizarre ice-skating accident story, but it was clear she didn't believe me. So I told her what had really happened, but not the details, and not about the nightmare of the recurring thoughts. These were things I couldn't talk about, not to ordinary people. Not to people I liked or cared about.

She wasn't shocked. Or if she was, she didn't show it. Instead she made me promise to ask her for help if I ever needed it. I promised, knowing that even if things did get bad, I wouldn't. It didn't work like that, not for me, not any more.

As I didn't want to go back on the dole, and now had some useful skills, I visited an employment agency. They looked at my resumé, asked me to take a typing test, and then said they'd be happy to put me on their books for temporary secretarial work. Was I happy to start on Monday? I'd had an interview for a real job, a permanent job, the previous week, but didn't feel confident about it, so I took up their offer.

Catching the 8.15 am train into town and turning up to work in a suit, my only suit, felt ridiculous. I was used to being able to wear jeans and boots. As I was a temp, no-one expected much from me, which was a good thing as I didn't actually know what a secretary did. Emily suggested that I just look in some of the files, and use old letters as templates. It would be easy, she said.

I spent three days sitting at a desk outside the chief legal counsel's office. The phone rang occasionally, he drafted a few emails to me, and I typed a few letters. Mostly I read a book. Nobody seemed to mind – or rather, nobody seemed to notice. I clearly didn't matter; I was invisible. After working at the magazine it was a shock, and when, on the final day, I had a call from one of the state's largest universities offering me a job, I accepted without a second thought.

It sounded fun. I'd be working on campus, writing, editing, proofreading and doing some design work. And, if what my new bosses had been wearing at the interview was any indication, I wouldn't have to invest in a new wardrobe. It would also give me time to get myself together, while I thought about what I really wanted to do. And could do.

I was worried that perhaps I just didn't have the stamina for a demanding job.

For the first few months, things went well. I worked, went out with my new colleagues, caught up with my old friends, and generally didn't push myself too hard. I felt, in fact, as though I were on holiday.

And then I did something foolish.

It had been over two years since I'd been involved with anyone. After Christian, I'd lost my nerve, and, as things had become more difficult, I'd lost interest in having a relationship at all. It was enough to have to cope alone.

With Alex it was easy. Too easy. He hadn't changed and neither had I: he still didn't want a relationship with me, just sex, and he still wanted to keep it a secret. I was still prepared to go along with this. We had both worked out, finally, that we weren't good for each other, indeed that we brought out the worst in each other, but this didn't matter. The familiarity did.

Around the same time, I was waiting for a train one day when I bumped into someone who I'd been at university with some years before. Kelly was house hunting, and as I was doing the same – having realised that I couldn't stay at my brother's indefinitely – we decided to find somewhere together.

After seeing a number of places that were good enough, if not perfect, and that I would have settled for, she found us one that was great. It was a renovated art deco unit in a security building, close to the harbour.

I'm not fundamentally lazy but I don't much like housework. Cleanliness is certainly important, but there's no need for obsessiveness about it. My childhood had been spent watching my mother constantly vacuuming and cleaning. A bench with crumbs on it was the enemy. It didn't matter whether it was hers or someone else's. When I'd lived in Sydney previously, I had let things slip a little from time to time. Sometimes, it was just too much to empty ashtrays, do the washing up or make the bed.

Sometimes it was more than that.

Early one morning, when I was going out with Patrick, my mother had arrived at my flat, unannounced. I was alone but unprepared. I had planned to tidy things a little, as I knew that the mess would upset her, but she was early.

She looked around, plainly appalled and I suggested that I took a quick shower. We could then go out for breakfast, there was no need to stay in the flat.

'I'll just pick up a few things for you while you do that,' she said.

I asked her not to, and promised that I'd just be a minute. Why didn't she just sit down on the sofa and read a magazine?

'No, no, I'd like to help,' she said, lifting up a towel from the bedroom floor.

'No . . .' I said, but it was too late.

Underneath the towel was a used condom.

Kelly, my new flatmate, reminded me of my mother. She cleaned and polished and tidied incessantly. Twice a week, while she was in the shower, she'd clean the tiles and polish the screen. I was always amazed that she didn't react to the bleach. The vacuum came out, it seemed, daily. And she cooked proper meals. As she was power-walking home from work, she'd call me on the mobile, ask what I'd like for dinner and would collect the ingredients from the supermarket. If people came over, there would be at least three courses.

In many ways Kelly was terrific to live with, and more than once I thought, this is what it must have been like to have a wife in the 1950s.

I did feel guilty about not doing my share of work, but we had different standards. I, for instance, refused to clean a surface that wasn't dirty, and I wasn't what she considered a good cook.

Ultimately though, the problem had nothing to do with household chores.

Kelly was a leggy, glamorous blonde. She spent money on her hair, her make-up, her clothes, her tan. And she knew she looked good.

When Alex dropped in, she'd flirt openly with him. Admittedly, she didn't know about our arrangement, but that didn't make it any easier to watch. Even this I could have tolerated though, if she hadn't misrepresented me.

It hadn't occurred to her that just because we'd both been to private schools, and the same university college, that we didn't think the same way or believe in the same things. Perhaps, when we were eighteen, we had been similar, but not anymore. I wasn't a Country Road-wearing Liberal voter, and hadn't been for a long time, not since I discovered what it was like to have no money. I didn't care what kind of car a person drove, and, shockingly, I wasn't even sure that I wanted to get married. Kelly had a good job, a good group of friends and was now ready for a good husband.

I think it was her certainty that really upset me. She felt that this was her right. Of course someone would want her, someone she loved. How could they not?

One evening, Kelly introduced me to a friend of hers, Jason. He was a journalist, outspoken, entertaining and friendly. When he asked me out I couldn't think of a reason to say no. I was sick of Alex's half-hearted attitude, and knew that it would have to end again sooner or later. It was a change to be in a position of control for once.

Jason and I started seeing each other regularly but I felt like the consolation prize. Kelly admitted she'd turned him down. By seeing me, he still got to see her – and she made sure he did. She'd tease him by lying supine on the couch in tiny shorts or wandering through the house in nothing but bathers, on the pretence of collecting a towel from the balcony.

It had taken me years to come to terms with the way my own body looked, and I didn't need this. Try as I might, it was hard to ignore the way Jason's eyes swivelled in the direction of her thighs. But I didn't say anything, not wanting to reveal my own insecurities.

Then I had an irregular Pap smear: I was told that I had a virus that was making the cells in my cervix mutate and these cells had to be removed. I was overcome with fear and guilt. Was this, I wondered, punishment for my promiscuity in the past? Had I brought it on myself?

I couldn't tell perfect Kelly. Instead I began to avoid her. I wasn't in the mood for upbeat conversations about her possible new boyfriends.

On top of this, I was bored at work. While the lack of pressure had at first been ideal, I now felt trapped. It wasn't challenging. It wasn't what I wanted to do.

Dr G was surprised to see me. It had been years since he'd advised me not to go to Adelaide. He was blunt. He wouldn't treat me unless I agreed to take an antidepressant. He would look for one with as few side effects as possible, and start me on a very low dose. If it didn't work, or I was uncomfortable, I could simply stop taking it – slowly.

I told him I didn't want to take anything that hadn't been properly tested. I was very nervous about taking anything at all, but if I had to compromise, then I wanted to be sure it was all right.

He laughed. He said he didn't prescribe anything that hadn't been properly tested. He then suggested Luvox, a Belgian drug in the same family as Prozac. I could begin taking it in the evenings. I was to see him again in a fortnight, when it should have started to kick in.

I went home, disappointed with myself. After a break of three years I was on antidepressants again. I didn't tell anyone. I didn't even want to admit it to myself, but the alternative possibility of slipping down again didn't bear thinking about. That night I took a quarter of a Luvox tablet. It was half what I'd been prescribed but I couldn't take any more.

A week or so later, I was lying on my bed reading when I overheard Kelly on the phone. She was speaking to Carol, with whom she'd become friendly: I wasn't sure what else they had in common, but they were certainly both tall and blonde.

'No. No better. Actually, she's bloody impossible. She's difficult, moody, and I don't know what I've done wrong. You know that I do everything around here. I cook. I clean. She should be grateful.' There was a pause. 'I think there's something going on though. I saw what looked like an X-ray envelope on her bed. She's going out with Jason but I'm pretty sure she's still sleeping with Alex. Do you think she might be pregnant?'

I couldn't listen to any more. I threw down my book, grabbed my wallet, and walked past a shocked-looking Kelly through the sitting room to the front door. Perhaps she hadn't realised I was there.

I returned after midnight, drunk and feeling slightly less upset. Emily had described Kelly as a 'fucking cow' enough times to take the sting away from the phone conversation I'd overheard.

The next morning I found a note. From time to time, we left notes for each other, about mundane things like phone messages or shopping list reminders. I thought perhaps the note was an apology. But no. It was an explanation. Apparently she didn't understand my moodiness and didn't know what to do about it. The truth was, she wrote, I frightened her.

I didn't know what to think. I certainly frightened myself sometimes but didn't realise that anyone else took any notice. None of my friends seemed to be frightened of me. I was the least confrontational person I knew. I didn't yell, I didn't throw things and I rarely even showed that I was angry. I couldn't understand what she was talking about. Was it my scars? Did she think they meant I was violent? It didn't occur to me then that she might have meant that she was frightened for me, not of me.

She'd said in a vague sort of way a few weeks previously that she was thinking about finding somewhere else to live. The birds outside her window were annoying her. At the time, I said nothing. The flat was in a great spot, had a reasonable rent, and was in walking distance of a lot of my friends. I didn't want to leave. And her complaint sounded rather pathetic.

After her note, and the telephone conversation, her comment about moving came back to me. Perhaps she was right. It was time to move again.

While I was at work that day, I received a phone call. It was about a job I'd applied for. They wanted to interview me. Various people at the company already knew me from my previous job in Melbourne, and they thought I'd be just right for this one. It would involve dealing with a number of tricky people, including the media, and it would be long hours and demanding. Did I want to come in for a chat?

Of course I did. Emily lent me a pinstriped suit, and I wore a T-shirt underneath. As I walked into the building, I crossed my fingers. It sounded just right.

A week later, I resigned from my position at the university. This was slightly more difficult than I had planned. I'd accepted the new job, and had promised to start in two weeks. This was the minimum notice I was allowed to give, according to my contract. Unfortunately, celebrating my new job involved getting very drunk. I managed to catch the train into work the following day without throwing up, but couldn't actually turn on my computer. Instead, I handed over my letter, dashed to the loo and went home to bed.

Coincidently, a flat I'd lived in before, in the next suburb, had just become available. It was as clean and light as I remembered, and I could afford it. Of course I shouldn't have taken it, but I somehow couldn't resist: I was being given another chance. It hadn't worked last time, but this time it would. While my friends all laughed, they were careful not to say I was mad.

Kelly hadn't seen this coming and after a flurry of notes, apologised, saying she realised that I was just depressed. If I'd only talk about it, she might understand and be able to help.

And she hadn't meant that she was going to leave me, but just the flat. She'd thought that we could both look for somewhere else, together.

But it was too late.

Jason had been on holiday overseas while all this was happening. He got back just as I was about to move.

'I'm sorry,' he said. 'If there's one thing I don't do, it's help people move.'

I was now 'people', was I? It didn't bode well.

A few days later, Jason came to visit, and I suggested we walk up to the local shops for coffee. The weather was warm, and I was feeling relaxed. I was away from Kelly, had a new job and the operation had been successful. The results were clear. I gave Jason a friendly hug – he pulled away. Initially, I said nothing, but while he talked about his trip and about meeting his extended family, I stewed.

By the time we got home I had decided to ask him what was going on. 'Why did you wait a week to call me when you got back from the UK?'

'No particular reason, I had a few other things on, I guess.' He shrugged.

I was furious, and confused. Before he left we'd seen each other regularly, and he constantly told me how gorgeous I was and how funny and clever. He liked being with me, he said, and I'd believed him. Even if I wasn't Kelly. I'd really looked forward to seeing him again, and, if the situation had been reversed, certainly would have called him straightaway.

I guessed what was going on, but wanted Jason to say it.

He looked around the flat, which was still untidy from the move. I wondered what he was looking for: an excuse? 'To be honest, you're a nice girl but, well, how should I put it – I can't see myself ever introducing you to my parents.'

I hadn't planned to introduce him to my parents either but then the only boyfriend of mine they'd ever met was Mike. And that hadn't gone well. Jason clearly wasn't someone who only went out with people he thought he'd marry, so his explanation was a cop out. It was also insulting. Combined with his refusal to help me move, and, even worse, his lack of interest in my health, it became obvious that his only interest was himself. But he was more than selfish: he'd revealed himself as an old-fashioned cad.

What Kelly had said about Alex was right. I was still seeing him. Not seriously, obviously, but it meant that I wasn't as upset about Jason's behaviour as I might have been. Alex, for once, had been behaving well. Emily had been away when I'd had the operation, which had been day surgery, so Alex had collected me from the clinic and cooked me dinner. He'd been unusually kind and considerate, and I realised that he was able to do this precisely because I was seeing Jason. Once the risk of commitment was removed, he could actually be nice to me.

I heard myself saying to Jason, 'Fine, thanks for clearing that up'. And then I opened the door, adding, as he left, that I wasn't really attracted to him anyway. I closed it before I could hear his response.

When I told my friends, their reactions varied. Peter had never liked him anyway. Emily said, 'Well, that's Kelly out of your life'. Alex just laughed.

It might have been the antidepressant that made the difference. Or it might have been the job, the flat and the clean bill of health. Whatever it was, things picked up again.

I had people over to dinner from time to time, even going as far as to produce meals from recipe books. And I started to buy some new clothes, finally shedding my depressed uniform of black and brown, second-hand cardigans, and ripped jeans. Initially, I felt self-conscious about colour but as I looked around at everyone else, it occurred to me that I was just as obvious – if not more – when I was trying to disappear. I bought a few more things, a tight T-shirt printed with a photograph of giraffes and a stripy see-through singlet. I bought some red pants. I even began painting my toenails, though not my fingernails – that would have been going too far.

In short, I began to enjoy being myself. I took up swimming. I gave up the Luvox, going off it so slowly that I had reduced the half-tablets to quarters again, before stopping altogether.

Things were even going well with Alex, who had taken to coming over and actually cooking.

Chapter Twenty-one

The new job was working out well. It was interesting, and it was challenging. It was in a slightly different area to where I'd worked before, but it was in publishing. Where I wanted to be.

I looked after politicians and essayists, as well as some well-known international fiction writers when they toured. Employed at a senior level because of my magazine experience, but having little knowledge of the way publicity worked, I made it up as I went along. This suited me, and seemed to suit everyone else.

If there was one thing I could do well, it was pretend.

What I didn't like was the office politics. Bitchiness was the order of the day, and the department was split in two: those who'd worked for the old boss who'd just retired, and those who'd been employed by the new one. I liked the new one, but even I could see that she wasn't coping, and was being constantly undermined.

The atmosphere was poisonous.

I could have dealt with this, if there hadn't been constant demands from every angle – the media, the publishers, the authors. It was a job that was never done, never good enough and it began to wear me down.

I kept reminding myself that I had done the right thing leaving Melbourne. The situation had been impossible and I hadn't imagined it. I hadn't.

Gradually, try as hard as I might to stop them, the same old symptoms began to return. I stopped wanting to go out or answer the phone when I was at home. And it was all I could do not to say 'fuck off' when I answered it at work. Ironing my clothes became too hard. And, worst of all, I began to think about harming myself again.

Constantly.

I'd take a walk around the block at lunchtime, to calm myself, and the images of knives, razors and blood would fill my head. There was no point seeing the doctor. I knew from experience that these thoughts weren't something he knew how to deal with, and I didn't want to take more drugs. I couldn't afford to have my thinking slowed down, or to be groggy. It hadn't been an issue when I'd been working at the university, as the job wasn't busy, and it didn't matter if I was a bit out of it.

In a publicity department, people might notice if I wasn't switched on.

Initially, I thought that maybe I could move to another position somewhere else within the company, which despite the politics, I liked. I spoke discreetly to a couple of people, but there was nothing permanent going that would suit me. There was part-time and freelance work available but the lack of a steady income worried me, and I didn't like the thought of being at home by myself too much.

My boss, unhappy herself, confidentially suggested that I'd be better off somewhere else. She too was thinking of leaving.

Reluctantly, I started looking.

Just as I was beginning to feel desperate, I saw a sales and marketing job advertised in a trade magazine. It would involve moving to the other side of the country. It was the perfect solution. Admittedly, I didn't know much about sales and marketing, but how hard could it be?

It would be a significant promotion, so wouldn't look as though I was running away. I wouldn't ever have to admit that I hadn't been coping.

And I wasn't seeing Alex anymore. One of his closest friends had died and he didn't want anything to do with me. Again.

When they offered me the job I accepted. There was nothing to keep me in Sydney, and I desperately hoped that leaving would be a good move.

Chapter Twenty-two

A month later, I was on a plane on my way to the most isolated capital city in the world. My friends and family were excited on my behalf as I'd made Perth sound like a fantastic place: relaxed, great beaches, cheap real estate, bachelors galore. They didn't know the real reason I was leaving. Only Emily was suspicious. 'Are you sure about this?' she'd said when I'd told her the news. Of course, I'd said, sounding more confident that I felt. I wasn't sure at all. I'd only ever been to Perth once before and hardly knew anyone. It also felt like my last chance. I'd moved so often.

This just had to work.

'Hello darling, how gorgeous to see you!' It was my mother's cousin, Annie, who I barely knew. She rushed out of the house as I pulled up in the taxi and gave me a hug and a kiss. It wasn't what I'd expected, and, while I was pleased, I was a little embarrassed. My side of the family rationed affection, and I'd done nothing to deserve this.

Annie went on to ask about the flight, my parents, my brothers, her family, and then offered me dinner.

Her house, where I was going to stay until I found somewhere of my own, was large and rambling, filled with a mixture of Persian rugs, antiques and furniture rescued from junk shops. There were paintings every-where. Large doors opened from the kitchen and the sitting room onto a back terrace and garden. It was already dark but the air was still warm, and faintly per-fumed.

Annie put a salad, some fresh bread, and some cold meat on a tray, and her husband Charles poured us some wine. We ate outside. After we'd eaten, Annie showed me my room.

'We go swimming at around 6.30 am. If you want to join us we'd love you to, otherwise, we'll see you for breakfast, and then Charles will give you a lift into work.'

I lay in bed that night, tossing and turning. Part of it was jet lag, part of it was excitement and part was fear. What if I couldn't do the job? How would I meet people? What if I hated Perth? No, I told myself, it would be fine. It was a chance to start again in a small and friendly city. The job would be great and less stressful than my last one. I'd have time to paint, to draw and to explore Western Australia.

I fell asleep feeling confident that I'd made the right decision.

As the very pregnant outgoing manager walked me through the files I began to feel anxious. This wasn't going to be straightforward. But she was adamant. 'If you have any questions don't hesitate to ring.' She'd read my resumé, and had been on the selection panel at the video interview. She knew that my sales and marketing experience was limited: why should I be embarrassed to call her if I needed to?

I arrived home at 6.30 pm, tired and conscious of what I'd taken on. It was a small office, and though I now had an assistant, I was going to be very busy.

On the upside, I now had a work car – with a V8 engine – and a very cute new pink Macintosh computer.

'You must be exhausted,' was the first thing I heard when I walked in. Annie then ordered me to lie down on the daybed in the corner of the kitchen, and rest while Charles made us both gin and tonics.

This is great, I thought, as I sipped my drink. I could really get used to this.

It took a month to find somewhere of my own to live, and during that time I got to know my Perth cousins. Things were different on this side of the Nullarbor. What really struck me was that they were all so friendly and affectionate. And open.

'That family secrecy,' said Annie one day, as we were driving towards a salvage yard to look for extra furniture. I'd moved into my own house by then and didn't have quite enough. 'I always hated it.'

Her own mother was infamous – and legendary – as she'd run away to Sydney at eighteen to become a journalist. After getting a job she had her hair bobbed and sent her mother her two long plaits in the post. It was a gesture I'd always admired.

She'd come back the following year and married, but remained outspoken and headstrong. Her daughters were the same.

Annie went on, 'They don't tell me anything – I didn't know you'd been sick for instance'.

Charles, a doctor, had noticed that I was on medication, and while not asking what it was for, suggested that if it was something I was taking regularly, then I should at least touch base with a local specialist. I'd told them both then that it was Tegretol, a mood stabiliser I'd been prescribed some years ago to treat manic depression. I admitted that I'd had a few problems in the past but didn't say that it was those same problems that had driven me across the country.

I was fine now, I told them. And I was.

I'd been fine since leaving Sydney. The move appeared to have done the trick.

'It's not as though it's something to be ashamed about, of course,' Annie had said. She wasn't at all like family.

The salvage yard was a treasure trove, and I found part of a kitchen cupboard that I could use as a bedside table. Meanwhile, Annie had found a piece of stainless steel to put on top of it. And I found a bookcase, and a door that I could put over a table frame to make a desk.

At home that night, I rang my mother, excited, and told her about the salvage yard and my finds.

'It's not old junk I hope. I rather hoped you'd got beyond that.' I gritted my teeth. She just couldn't move on, could she? She just couldn't get over the fact that I'd once lived in a warehouse and had worn damaged, second-hand clothes. After I'd left Melbourne, she remained on edge, seeing me as unpredictable, someone who was, at any moment, about to do something embarrassing. It meant that every conversation was fraught.

How long would it take to be forgiven?

I wished she were more like Annie. And then felt disloyal. She was my mother after all, and she didn't mean things to be this way. Still, it was nice to be on the other side of the country and have a desert between us.

For less than the price of a small one-bedroom flat in inner city Sydney, I was able to rent a whole house in inner city Perth. Built in the 1940s, it had two bedrooms, one that I could use as a study. In the sitting room there was a large window overlooking a park. The park came with a lake and swans. Black swans. There was a small garden in the front, and, at the back, an ivy-covered garden shed.

A week after putting down a rental deposit, my furniture had been delivered. My bed, an antique I'd bought in a junk shop in Melbourne years ago, had a homemade base. I'd sticky-taped pine slats to the side rails. It was always meant to be a temporary measure, but somehow, I'd never got around to fixing it properly. Now seemed the right time. I looked at the base again and realised that if I anchored two boards on the rails, I could then secure the slats to them. I borrowed an electric drill and completed the job.

Fixing my bed had been simple – everything that seemed to be difficult elsewhere was easy in Perth. Work was only five minutes away by car and the closest shopping centre, Subiaco, had cafés, a supermarket and a cinema. My cousins were only ten minutes down the road.

I began going to gallery exhibitions, found clothes shops I liked, and generally enjoyed exploring the place.

I tried not to think about the fact that I still didn't really know anyone who wasn't related to me.

I didn't want to impose on the cousins of my own age, who, despite being friendly, were busy. Similarly, my work mates, while pleasant, didn't show any interest in doing anything outside work hours. They had their own lives. I could have asked them to introduce me to people when I first arrived, could have explained that I knew no-one. But I didn't want them to think that I wasn't settling in, or that I wasn't able to meet people by myself.

As far as everyone was concerned then, I was happy. I liked my own company and was getting along well. I wasn't lonely, I told myself. Only old ladies got lonely. In fact, things were going well. I had a real house, a real car and a real job. I had all the things an adult should have. It occurred to me that I actually was an adult: it was a frightening thought. I wasn't ready yet. I hadn't worked things out. I wasn't poised, elegant, assured. I still felt like an awkward seventeen-year-old in many ways, and was in fact often still mistaken for a student. But I wasn't and hadn't been for years. I was now over 30. Many of my friends were married, and had businesses, or serious jobs. Many of them were happy.

Every time I spoke to Emily, or my old university friend Dee, I put the phone down feeling slightly depressed. They, to me, seemed to be living. Emily was now in Tokyo, going to nightclubs until 5 am, flying over to Hong Kong for weekends. Dee was an architect living with the man she loved in Bondi. Even Catherine, who I still remembered as a child with mulberry stains through her hair, was an economist, now married and living in London. Peter was a corporate solicitor.

Everyone, it seemed, was thriving. I felt a sense of frustration. Why couldn't I thrive? What kept me from engaging with life? Even when I was content, I often felt removed, as though I were watching everyone else through a sheet of glass.

I was determined to make things work. I joined a gym and started attending life drawing classes. The key, I decided, was to do things that I enjoyed. A character in *Good Morning Midnight*, a Jean Rhys novel used the phrase 'my little life'. It seemed to be an apt one. Perhaps that's all it was. Perhaps I was wrong to want something more; perhaps there wasn't anything more. Maybe this was how it was for everyone, and I was simply being unreasonable. The thing was, I'd tried everything: drugs, moving, changing jobs, changing clothes, losing weight – but I always ended up in the same place.

Whenever anyone asked me, I told them I was doing well. Increasingly, I made phone calls to my friends in the east, and even to my parents. I tried to avoid the enveloping sense of isolation.

There was another reason for not feeling as happy as I might. The job, which had started off difficult, was becoming more so by the day. I didn't want to bother my predecessor, who'd by now had her baby, so I tried to muddle through. The one person who could have helped didn't. He worked for me, but was too busy white-anting, and being bitter, to offer useful advice. He resented my age, sex and most of all my obvious inexperience, and made no secret of it. If he found a typo somewhere, say in a flyer, he'd fax it to me, and often to my boss as well. It reached the point where every time I did something, I was nervous. Even the things I knew I could do with my eyes closed, such as organising launches or publicity, became stressful and difficult. I began to actively hate going into the office. It seemed that everyone except my assistant and my boss wanted me to resign, but I couldn't do it.

I knew I'd made the wrong decision in accepting the job in the first place but I was determined to stick it out. I'd made a commitment and I couldn't bear the thought of admitting that I'd made yet another mistake. You can move only so many times before people start to notice and ask questions and I couldn't afford for anyone to start asking questions.

My solution was to get fit.

Going to the gym gave me something to look forward to after work, and somewhere to go. It was either that, or go home and drink. I thought the gym would be less dangerous – I was wrong.

One morning, I woke up, as usual, and tried to sit up. As I did so, I became aware of the most excruciating pain in my neck. I lay down again and moved my toes, my legs, my arms. They were all fine. It was just my neck. I tried again, without success, to get out of bed. It hurt too much. Something had happened; I'd felt a crick the evening before when I'd been at a circuit training class, but had ignored it.

Deciding there couldn't be anything really wrong with me, I made another attempt to get up, thinking that if I did it quickly, it might hurt less. It didn't, but the pain didn't last as long. I walked slowly towards the bathroom. Perhaps a shower would help. It didn't, but by moving very carefully, I was able to work out which positions hurt and which were manageable. If I stayed perfectly still, for example, I could avoid the pain. Somehow, by making careful use of the car's mirrors, I managed to drive myself to work.

It didn't occur to me to stay home.

As I tried to lie down that night, I realised that it wasn't going to happen. I was better off sleeping upright on the couch. So, after finding a quilt and another pillow, I settled down for the evening. It was a very long night, as every time I moved in my sleep, I was woken up with a blast of pain.

It was no better by the next day – worse if anything – so I rang Annie to find out if she could recommend a doctor. (Charles was a research scientist, and hadn't actually treated anyone for years.)

I had seen a GP when I'd first arrived and needed a new prescription for Tegretol. He'd asked a few questions, and then said, 'So why do you think you want to hurt yourself?'

I sat there, thinking it was a rhetorical question, and waiting for him to tell me. There was a few minutes' silence, and then it dawned on me that he was actually waiting for me to answer. 'I don't know.'

Stress exacerbated the urge, but I didn't know why I wanted to do it in the first place.

He then asked if I was religious.

It was an odd question. I told him that I'd been brought up as an Anglican, but that it wasn't something I thought about.

He had a theory about the link between self-harm and religion, but said it was just a theory. Hardly even that. Just that there might be a link.

Historically, yes, there was, of course. I thought of hairshirts and self-flagellation. But I thought he was missing the point. I didn't tell him, but I thought that if there was a link, it wasn't to do with belief, but guilt.

He wrote out the prescription and I decided not to see him again.

The doctor Annie recommended practised a mixture of traditional and alternative medicine. He felt around my neck and said that he didn't think it warranted an X-ray. Not yet. Anti-inflammatories and rest should do it.

'Aside from the neck, how are you feeling?' he asked. While I'd waited in the reception area, I'd filled in the required form, giving a few details of my medical history. He now had this in front of him. 'It must be tough coming over here by yourself from the east. How are you settling in? Have you met many people?'

'Not really.' It was embarrassing but true.

'You've obviously got a history of depression. You don't have any concerns about that at the moment, do you? Moving is a big thing.'

I took a deep breath. 'I'm fine. I want to drive my car into a brick wall, but otherwise I'm fine.' Until I uttered those words, I hadn't realised that was how I felt. I was shocked.

The doctor was calm. 'Okay. Are you thinking about doing that any time soon?'

'I can't drive well enough at the moment.' I smiled.

'Actually, you shouldn't be driving at all.' He paused. 'Have you felt like doing something like this before?'

I wasn't sure. I'd felt miserable, depressed, melancholy, destructive and angry but had I ever coldly, seriously contemplated giving up entirely? I'd taken too many pills, but that was because I needed a rest from myself. And I had driven into another car – but no, despite it all, I hadn't.

This was a new development.

The truth was I felt possessed. I could cope with depression – I didn't like it, but could deal with it. What I couldn't deal with was not having control of my mind. And that's what had happened.

I admitted, finally, and with huge relief, that I felt like cutting myself constantly: at work, when I woke up, when I was watching television, when I was driving, eating, showering. All the time. Visions of blood dripping down my forearms, of smeared knives, of used razors, of jagged wounds all collided with each other. The more I tried to put them out of my head, the more insistent they became. They were vivid and vicious.

They had also reached a new level of intensity and I was distraught. After all, they were what I had been running from for so many years now. They were why I left so many houses, so many cities. It was as though they had always been waiting for me here in Perth, and it was only a matter of time before I arrived and they found me alone, defenceless.

Part of me – and it was getting stronger daily – was convinced that the only way to stop them was to give in. To get a knife and get it over with. I knew the reason the thoughts were so persistent was because I wasn't giving in.

All I needed to do was let go.

But if I started again, I wouldn't be able to stop. I'd held off now for five years but just didn't know what to do. I didn't want to live this way anymore. I couldn't. I just wanted them to stop and, apparently, was prepared to do whatever was necessary to make that happen.

'I think we need to get you in to see a psychiatrist asap,' said the doctor. While he was looking in his address book, he asked what kind of treatment I'd had in the past.

'Not a lot, not really. Drugs.' I listed them. 'A bit of group therapy while I've been in hospital from time to time but nothing else.'

'Have you ever had any cognitive behavioural therapy?'

I didn't even know what it was.

'I think you'd really respond to it,' he said.

Then he made an appointment for the following week for me with a psychiatrist who had a practice around the corner. I was to go back and see him in two days' time. 'If you need to come in before then, just let me know. Here's my card,' and he wrote another number on the back. 'That's my mobile. Call any time.'

As I left, he called out behind me, 'Do send my best to Annie and Charles when you next see them'.

Annie later told me he'd been to uni with one of her sons.

By the time I got home, I was exhausted. Admitting that I felt like I did meant that I also would have to confront the question of why. Now 31, I realised that if I didn't work it out soon, my life wasn't ever going to get better. I would never be happy if I didn't confront it. Whatever 'it' was.

And what kind of therapy was he talking about anyway? Surely if it was something that was going to work, someone would have suggested it before?

While the stiffness and the acute pain that shot from my neck whenever I moved were disabling, they also brought intense relief. For a few precious days I was spared my mental torment and I had a chance to think about what I wanted, rather than just coping, from hour to hour.

I knew that I didn't have long and that this was just a window of respite. It was like the intermission in a film. The images would be back, probably worse, once my body began to mend.

Chapter Twenty-three

Dr P was the seventh psychiatrist I'd visited, so I didn't walk into his room expecting miracles. Nevertheless, a tiny part of me thought that maybe, just maybe, there was something that everyone else had missed.

Could I just take a pill and make it all go away? Was it that easy? No, no, it wasn't. I'd been given antipsychotics before and they didn't stop anything. They just made me very tired – too tired to want to cut myself. That wasn't a long-term solution. Besides, I wasn't psychotic. It felt like madness certainly, but I knew it wasn't.

But what is madness, if not being able to control your own mind?

If there were a cure, then there would be chapters in textbooks, and articles in journals. The medical professional would know about it and I wouldn't have spent ten years ricocheting around, from doctor to doctor, place to place, trying to escape it.

As I sat in the waiting room and watched the wall clock tick over, I contemplated walking out. The appointment had been scheduled for 10 am, and it was now nearly half-past. What if, like everyone else, he couldn't do anything and I was condemned? I didn't know if I could cope with being told that. It was almost easier not to know, and so still be able to hope.

I made an effort to hold back tears.

Finally, Dr P opened the door and asked me to come in. He was tall, with short, prematurely grey hair. Reassuringly, he was wearing a black suit and T-shirt – perhaps he really wasn't going to be like the others. Before he even had time to introduce himself, I started to cry. He offered me the box of tissues from the coffee table in the centre of the room, then wait-ed for me to calm down. He wasn't in any hurry.

After a few minutes, the sobbing subsided and I was able to breathe normally. I looked around the room, which was tastefully decorated in shades of red and green with dark wooden furniture. A large win-dow looked out onto a garden. He was the first psychi-atrist I'd visited who actually had a couch. I'd chosen to sit on the edge of an armchair opposite it. I had developed a habit of sitting on the edge of furniture, as though poised for a quick escape. He asked me what I was smiling at.

The couch, I told him. It seemed so, so New York, so Woody Allen.

He told me it had been there when he arrived, and then he changed the subject. He wanted to know about me – and what I was doing there.

I told him. I told him about the images, and the urges, about the hospitals, the bouts of depression, the alcohol, the eating problems, and the moving. As I talked I became more and more despondent, more convinced that he couldn't help. All psychiatrists were the same: what had I been thinking?

'Do you actually want to be helped? You don't seem to want to be here,' he asked.

That wasn't fair. 'It's not that – well it is, in a way. I've just seen so many doctors, shrinks, registrars, you name it, and none of them have been able to help. I've just had it, and I don't know what to do anymore.' I clenched my jaws so I didn't start crying again.

He nodded and then looked at me over the top of his glasses.'I think I can help you but you'll have to cooperate, otherwise there's nothing I can do. We'd both be wasting our time.' He looked at his file notes, 'You're what, 31? And you've been having problems, of one sort or another, for at least fifteen years. If you don't do something now, you'll suddenly find that you've reached 40 and nothing will have changed.'

What he said was true. 'I don't want that,' I said quietly.

'Then we need to work together to ensure that doesn't happen. There's an excellent clinic about five minutes from here.'

He made it sound like a restaurant. If I agreed, people would know I wasn't well, and, as it had happened before, they'd assume it would happen again. And again. I had managed to stay out of mental hospitals for three and a half years now. Besides, I had a job, I paid my bills, I cooked myself dinner. I was functioning well. Psychiatric hospitals were for those suffering from psychiatric problems. Despite sitting in a psychiatrist's rooms, despite admitting that I couldn't cope with the images in my head and that I wanted to drive my car into a brick wall, I didn't see myself as mentally ill.

He tried to reassure me. It wasn't a public hospital but a private clinic, it had world-class intensive treatment programs, and it was extremely comfortable. Why didn't I just pop round and have a look at it after our appointment? If I didn't like it then I didn't have to stay there. He just thought it would be the best thing for me at the moment – and there was a CBT course they ran that would be good for me.

The referring doctor had mentioned CBT as well. I asked him what it was, and he filled me in.

The theory behind CBT, or cognitive behavioural therapy, is simple: your thinking and your underlying beliefs – which you might not even be aware of – can affect your mental health. They can actually make you sick. CBT is apparently particularly useful for treating eating disorders, depression, anxiety disorders and obsessive-compulsive disorders. A real benefit is that the patient can start making changes immediately, and going over traumatic events or relationships isn't necessary. Sometimes there is no one thing that makes a person behave in a certain way. I certainly couldn't think of anything that made me the way I was, and had never been able to. It had always bothered me, and I had somehow felt that discovering the trigger for my behaviour would provide the cure. This was, apparently, a long way from the truth.

Dr P then suggested that I start on a course of antidepressants. The Tegretol wasn't enough, it only took out the peaks and troughs, and though it probably meant that I wasn't as bad as I could have been, it wasn't an antidepressant.

I put my foot down. 'I can't.' My medication phobia had returned to the extent that I couldn't even take the anti-inflammatories prescribed for the pain in my neck. It was ironic: I was thinking about carving up my arms or writing myself off in a car but was nervous about side effects caused by medication. 'Besides,' I told him, 'I'm not depressed'. And I didn't believe I was. Unhappy, yes; depressed, no.

He didn't argue but told me an antidepressant would be useful. There were many different kinds to choose from now, but there was one particular sort, Cipramil, that he thought I'd respond well to. It had very few side effects, though he suggested that I not read the accompanying leaflet.

We reached a compromise. I'd look at the clinic, and, if I didn't think it was too awful, would check in the next day and start on the CBT program on Monday. The alternative was to stay at home, and at work, and see him once a week. But I knew that it wasn't a realistic option – besides, an intensive course would kick-start the therapy process. Once in the clinic, he'd start me on a very low dose of Cipramil, which would be gradually increased until I reached what he called a therapeutic dose.

After ensuring that a bed was, in fact, available, he gave me the address of the clinic.

As I was walking out I said to him, 'Do you know what I'm really terrified of? The wrong side winning. It's as though my mind has split in two and I have no control over it. And the thing is, I'm beginning to get confused about which side is right and which is wrong.'

'That's why I think that you really should be in hospital for a bit, and the CBT will really help,' he said. 'Trust me. You might not feel as though you have any control now, but you have a lot more than you think.'

Chapter Twenty-four

I'd told my boss that I had 'women's problems' and would be away for a couple of weeks. It wasn't really a lie, I did have problems and I was a woman after all. It also meant that everyone was too embarrassed to ask any more questions.

Once, I'd been able to use my job – whatever, wherever, it was – as a defence against any intrusive and violent thoughts. I couldn't any longer, so it was better not to be in the office at all. I'd already spent weeks just staring at my computer screen, or rearranging increasingly large piles of papers. I'd put off as many decisions as possible, not because I didn't trust my judgment, but because I just couldn't make them. Everything, even simple things, was too difficult. I'd avoided speaking to my colleagues where possible, and left notes for my assistant. Phone calls and emails had gone unanswered. And it was only a matter of time before someone else noticed that I wasn't coping – and what then? The thought of people discovering that there was something wrong terrified me. So far, I'd always been able to keep my problems out of my professional life.

Annie and Charles were sympathetic when I told them I was going in to the clinic for a short stay. A couple of weeks, I said. I didn't tell them what the matter was, only that I wasn't feeling well. I couldn't tell them about the thoughts or the urge to hurt myself, as I didn't want to upset them. They had been so kind to me, and, somehow, it felt like I'd let them down.

Melissa, who was now Archie's wife and my sister-in-law, was shocked when she heard. 'I'll come over,' she said immediately. 'This isn't something you should go through alone.'

'I'll be fine,' I told her. I said she needn't worry, it was a long way to come. 'I'll be fine,' I repeated, as I had so many times before.

'Vic, you're not fine,' she said. 'You wouldn't be being admitted to a psychiatric hospital if you were.' Her parents lived in Perth, it was a good opportunity to visit them too, she could catch up with friends – it wouldn't be a problem at all.

Suddenly I did want her to be there. I didn't want to go through it alone, yet again. It felt uncomfortable, but I struggled against the feeling, and said, 'Actually, that'd be great'.

Melissa had suffered from chronic fatigue syndrome several years earlier: was this why she seemed to understand what I was going through? Perhaps it was a bond, that feeling of being judged by so many as a malingerer, or of not trying. She knew what it was like to suffer from something that others didn't see, and that some didn't even believe in.

She said she'd organise a flight and be over in a few days.

After I put down the phone, I realised that this was what I'd been missing for years – a family member who didn't judge me, who simply wanted to be there. Friends had always been wonderful, but as I'd got older I'd stopped relying on them and increasingly kept silent. It wasn't fair to lean on them, time and time again – they had their own lives to lead and, now, their own families or partners. Also, there was that niggling feeling that I should have 'this', whatever 'this' was, sorted out by now.

I hadn't acknowledged until that moment how difficult it had been over the last few years, keeping it all to myself. At least, when I'd been openly sick, I could talk about it openly. Pretending to be well had made things so much worse.

'Comfortable' was an understatement when it came to describing the clinic. A two-storey red brick building, it had a neat garden at the front with a fountain in the middle. It was what I imagined an exclusive health resort would be like, although, as I quickly discovered, there were no swimming pools, saunas or tennis courts. What I particularly liked was that it didn't feel like a hospital, and none of the patients were locked in.

My room wasn't large but had its own bathroom, television and desk under a window looking out over the street. There was an information sheet on the desk with details about the washing machines, the meal times and the video library.

That first night I went to bed at nine, after nervously taking my first dose of antidepressants in some time. I rationalised it: if something went wrong, I was at least in a hospital.

Although the room was quiet and the bed wasn't too hard, it was difficult to sleep. There was a plastic sheet over the mattress, which meant that it was impossible not to sweat, and the nurse shone a torch in at eleven and asked if I was awake. For the first few days I was indeed awake every time. Wide awake at eleven, and one, and three. I couldn't sleep but refused to take any sleeping pills – it was difficult enough to agree to the Cipramil, let alone something else. Besides, they weren't a habit I wanted to get into and there had to be a point at which I'd get so tired that I'd just have to sleep.

After a week I was indeed sleeping soundly but yawning constantly in the morning, at lunchtime, in the afternoon, and even while I was in bed at night. Eventually, I worked out that the yawning wasn't anything to do with tiredness, but was a side effect of the medication. If this was to be the only one, I thought, then I wasn't doing too badly.

As for the CBT, that was a different matter altogether.

Chapter Twenty-five

The CBT course meant spending two weeks, from nine to five, Monday to Friday, in a room with seven other depressed, obsessed and anxious people. The first morning, we were told that cognitive behavioural therapy was about understanding that emotions, thoughts and beliefs were all connected. The way we thought, as well as what we thought, could make us feel better – or worse.

We were given folders with worksheets and exercises to do. We talked about balances, strategies, resources and support networks, as well as looking at how to identify styles of thinking, such as black and white, over-generalisation, jumping to conclusions, and catastrophising.

Very quickly we learnt that the key to CBT was not to trust our instincts. For me, this was the hardest part.

Once, several years ago, I'd been spending a few days with my parents. It was during the time that things in my life had been going unusually well. I was living in Melbourne, loving my work, and they were proud of me.

We were at the dinner table talking about what we'd done during the day. I'd been in the bank, and was chatting to the teller when her face went pale and her jaw, literally, dropped. I turned around to see two men with sawn-off shotguns and balaclavas running through the door. They yelled, 'Get down,' and, as the only customer, I did so. So did the bank staff.

After they'd left, a woman came down from upstairs from the administration section. 'It was worse for us,' she said, shaking her head. 'We couldn't do anything.'

Everyone at the table had laughed at this story, and the fact that I'd almost parked-in the getaway van. Illegally. (The police kindly agreed not to give me a ticket.) We then moved on to the next event, the next story, and the robbery wasn't mentioned again.

I hardly ever think about it now. I don't like men in tracksuit pants and balaclavas, but then I never did.

In terms of the CBT course, it showed clearly how I'd been taught to deal with anything that was unpleasant: make light of it, then forget about it. Or, if that proved difficult, then force yourself to forget about it. Don't give in to anything, especially emotions. 'Rise above it,' was our mantra.

This technique seemed to work for my parents, and had sometimes worked for me, but had its dangers, as I finally began to learn.

When we were asked to write an honest list of self-criticisms I was surprised by what I actually wrote down. I felt lazy, overweight, boring, untidy, ungrateful, unmotivated, unable to concentrate and unhappy.

Clearly I hadn't successfully dealt with the way I felt about myself by ignoring it. Ignoring something, and dealing with it, were not the same thing at all but for some reason I struggled with this concept.

What was wrong with a coping strategy of not thinking about something?

And what did all this have to do with the bloody images? I was getting impatient, as I just couldn't see the connection.

Ray, one of the therapists, had firm ideas about it. 'Don't you think that these images, these urges, that are making your life so difficult, may be a result of your beliefs or thoughts?'

No, I replied. The thoughts came out of nowhere.

Ray shook his head. 'I disagree, but let's put the issue of the images aside for the moment.'

It was easy for him to say. They'd lessened since I'd been admitted to hospital, but they hadn't gone away.

The first few days of CBT didn't make me feel better, but worse. I had arrived with what I thought was one problem, and then uncovered a whole lot more. Most disturbingly, my whole approach to dealing with life was being questioned and I really didn't like it.

As I lay in bed one night, tossing, turning and yawning, I remembered the doctor's letter in which I'd been described as having illogical thought patterns. At the time I'd been insulted. I was many things, but I wasn't, I thought, stupid. But CBT wasn't about intelligence, or lack thereof: it was about unlearning bad habits. Like a lot of people, I was rather attached to my bad habits. They were comfortingly familiar, if nothing else.

The intensive nature, small size and specialised structure of this course meant that it was unlike any group therapy I'd done before. Previously, in other hospitals, I'd got the feeling that 'groups' were something aimed at keeping patients busy and I'd gone because I had nothing better to do, not because I thought they might actually help.

Here we even had homework, often set by other patients, who were also members of the group. During the first week, when I was set the task of writing down all my self-criticisms, I was also asked to write about my expectations, and how I could lower them. I'd sat at the desk in my room after dinner at around 6.30 pm, feeling frustrated. There was nothing wrong with my expectations of myself and I didn't want to lower them. That was giving in. I wrote: 'If I were to lower them I would feel disappointed in myself'. I knew that this wasn't what I was supposed to do, I was supposed to say that if I wasn't so hard on myself, so demanding, that I'd feel better, less stressed. Something though, made me want to argue. Similarly, when it came to the second half of the exercise, writing down my good qualities, I left the section blank.

The following day, the blank section caused an uproar. None of the other patients agreed with me. Of course I had good qualities, everyone did. I was caring, kind – they'd seen this already. Why hadn't I written anything?

Why indeed? I wasn't sure entirely, only that I didn't feel that I had any good qualities. Or rather, that none were good enough. Nothing I did or said was good enough but I couldn't make anyone understand the way I felt. The conversation moved into a discussion about how it was impossible to be perfect, to expect over 100 percent of yourself. It was illogical.

I felt trapped: wasn't it normal to want perfection? Even if you knew you couldn't achieve it?

Claire, the other therapist, asked me why I wanted to hurt myself.

I didn't know. I still didn't know.

She tried again, was there a trigger? Did something make the thoughts happen? Surely I didn't have them all the time?

There was something. 'Stress makes them worse.'

One of the other patients then interrupted. 'It seems pretty simple to me. If you didn't have such high expectations, you wouldn't feel so stressed when they're not met, and then wouldn't want to harm yourself.' Problem solved.

How could I make them understand that if I lowered my expectations, it would lead to feeling disappointed in myself, and feeling miserable. I didn't want to work as a checkout chick for the rest of my life just to avoid stress. One of the other patients pointed out that checkout chicks also often got quite stressed with long queues and rude customers.

I hadn't kept going to this point to drop out again anyway: I'd tried that before and it didn't work. There had to be another way.

Claire stepped in again. What was stress anyway? It could be a reaction to one thing or to many, and it could be a reasonable reaction. It could motivate you, as well as incapacitate you. Everyone had ideas about this, and the focus moved away from me for a time.

But the conversation had made me uncomfortable. I wasn't ready to admit it yet, but there was something in what they were all saying. Increasingly, I was getting the feeling that I might have somehow been making things much, much harder for myself.

Although I kept saying – daily – that the program wasn't dealing with my problem, I knew that it was. The urge to hurt myself didn't spring, fully formed, from nowhere. It was a response, and while recognising this was helpful for me, it wasn't enough. What I needed was to understand my thought processes, understand where they came from: once I knew this, perhaps I could control them.

When the idea of 'positive affirmations' came up, I shook my head. I refused to look in the mirror in the morning and tell myself, in a perky voice, that things were great, that I was great, that the world was a good place. It was ridiculous. Besides, I was beginning to wonder if I should ever believe anything I told myself. So far the most important thing I'd learnt in this course was that I wasn't to be trusted.

Ray was ready when I said that this wasn't going to work for me. 'Just choose the ones from the list that make sense to you, and forget about those that don't. You're right, they aren't any use to you if you don't believe them.'

I didn't believe any, so skipped the exercise, but as a concession I agreed to try to stop criticising myself.

The images had worried me for so many years that until the course, I hadn't even noticed I had an internal critic as well. The blood and violence demanded attention but the voice was insidious. As I got dressed in the morning, I'd look at my thighs. 'Fat thighs,' said the voice. If I answered a question wrong, 'Stupid idiot' said the voice, if I dropped something the voice would say quietly, 'Clumsy cow'. It gave a running commentary on exactly what I was doing wrong, every day, all day.

Was this really 'constructive criticism' or something else? For years I'd listened as my mother told us how fat she was, how pathetic, how weak. She was an idiot, she said, and a fool. She was none of those things – quite the opposite in fact, but I'd grown up believing that was how everyone thought about themselves. Recognise your faults, and you'll be better, stronger for it; criticise yourself before anyone else gets the chance. This, to me, was normal – so normal that I'd forgotten I was doing it at all.

Chapter Twenty-six

At the end of the first week, I began to cry and cry and cry. Embarrassed to be seen doing so in the dining room, I'd rush up to my room, or go outside. If I felt tears coming on during the sessions, I'd lash out at one of the therapists. It was their fault I was feeling like this – their fault and the fault of my psychiatrist, Dr P – and I was furious with them all. More than that, I was beginning to understand that I'd spent years suffering unnecessarily. I wasn't cured yet but I knew now that it was possible.

By the time Melissa arrived on the following Tuesday, I was starting to feel better. The course was having an effect and it did make a difference not having to go into the office, or cook, clean or iron. The antidepressants were also beginning to kick in. My mood, which I had grown used to and thought as normal, had definitely improved. I couldn't believe that I hadn't even realised I had been depressed this time.

Melissa brought with her flowers and magazines, the standard kind of presents that people bring to hospital patients. She was also interested in how I was, and whether the treatment was working. She came to the family session, and asked the therapists for reading material.

Archie, meanwhile, had been ringing every second day, and even Jeremy, my ever elusive younger brother, had rung.

My parents didn't know what had happened and initially I had decided not to tell them. They must have known that things hadn't been going well, as I'd been ringing them a lot, which was out of character. But I hadn't said I was unhappy, so perhaps they really hadn't picked up on it. Or didn't want to. I'd certainly not admitted to any problems since leaving Melbourne. I'd finally learnt then that it was better not to: they couldn't help me and they didn't understand. Their priorities and mine were very different. They wanted me to have a good job, a family and buy a house. I wanted to survive.

My mother would see this new hospitalisation as an example of how I was weak and irresponsible. What would my boss say? Had I thought about that? What about everyone else? My cousins, the family? Did I only ever think about myself?

I was relieved when my father was told, and called me. I wasn't up to defending my decisions to my mother. When she finally did call, it was a short conversation. I didn't tell her what I'd decided to do.

Just prior to the end of the program, those of us who were staying in hospital were asked to spend time at home, to help ease us back into normal life. This was a very sensible thing as it was surprising how quickly you became institutionalised.

My house was half an hour away. I was in no hurry so walked slowly, stopped at a café, and took nearly double that time to get there. As I turned the corner I could see that the house next door had now been fully demolished. It had been vacant for several months and then I'd come home from work one evening, just before going into hospital, to find bulldozers there. Luckily all my windows had been shut but my garden along the fenceline was covered in rubble, as were my front steps.

I unlocked the door and was greeted with a musty smell. Nervous about leaving my windows open too far, I hadn't ever been able to get rid of it, even when I was at home. One of the things I'd not known about Perth, until I moved there, was that it had one of the highest crime rates in the country. The news always seemed to be full of theft and violent break-ins. My assistant's house had been broken into twice in the last six weeks. The second time she'd been at home and the intruder, seeing her, had continued walking in. It wasn't until he noticed her boyfriend that he turned and ran.

After putting some clean clothes in my backpack, I went to the kitchen and made a pot of coffee. Sitting down at the kitchen table, I began to understand how much I hated living there. The house was large and light, but it was also empty and cold.

The neighbour's dog was barking, as usual. It barked nonstop, day and night, and had done since I'd moved in. One morning, after yet another evening lying there thinking of ways to strangle it, I'd complained to the owner. She brightly told me that one of the other neighbours had also asked her to do some-

211

thing about it, so she was going to get a sedative from the vet. The poor little thing, I knew how it felt.

I locked the door behind me, dreading having to return. Not just to the house but to the job and life that went with it. It had been my decision to move to Perth, and I'd gone hoping that things would be better. The eighteen months left in my contract stretched relentlessly before me. But it wasn't a prison sentence, I thought as I walked back to the clinic, there was no reason that I shouldn't just leave and go back to Sydney. The more I thought about it, the more excited I became. I'd resign, pack up my things, and go back east. It might be admitting defeat but if I was better already, then surely that was a win? Couldn't I just look at it as cutting my losses? As a failed experiment?

During the next morning's session I discovered that I wasn't the only one who had found going home difficult but I was the only who planned to move as a result. There was another member of the group who was from Sydney, and who found Perth a difficult place to meet people but, unlike me, he wasn't alone. He was happily married, with children. While his kids were enjoying their new school, his wife her new job, he was missing his friends, the local RSL, his Saturday golf game.

As part of the program was to try to help other members of the group with their problems, we asked if he had been out in Perth, if he'd joined a golf club. His answer was no. And it quickly became obvious that he wasn't actually trying to make new friends but expected them to find him.

There were similarities in our situations, but unlike this man, I had a choice. No-one was going to care if I left.

Ray wasn't impressed with my solution. I still wasn't dealing with my problems apparently. I was running away. Again. Doing what he called 'a geographical'. (There was actually a name for it.) He went on, reminding me about what I'd told them all. How many times I'd moved in the past, and how it hadn't worked. I couldn't run away from myself. This was my opportunity to break my habit, and to settle down.

But I knew this time that it wasn't about running away, it was about going home. We'd been asked at one point to do a 'map' of the people we felt made up our support networks. Mine were in Melbourne and Sydney. When I'd been asked to do it again, without factoring in the phone, there wasn't much to it.

Ray was adamant. I could build a network in Perth. I could use the other people in the program as a start, and expand.

Everyone agreed. And I didn't need to stay by myself if I didn't want to. Other people in the course said I could have dinner with them, or visit them. Two of the women even said I could stay with them if I wanted. I didn't need to be alone.

'Running away isn't the answer.' He'd made his point, but Ray couldn't help repeating himself.

That evening, I had a visit from my psychiatrist.

He'd been speaking to Ray. What was this about moving back to Sydney?

I told him. I'd rather be with family and friends, and, if necessary, poor and unemployed for a while,

than stay in Perth. It was a long, long way from anywhere. A six-hour flight from Sydney, or three-day
drive – if you didn't stop on the way. He nodded. If I
felt it was the right thing to do, and that I would genuinely be happier, then I should go. He knew about
the 'geographicals' but was more concerned about me.
I would be isolated again once I left hospital. I understood more about how my mind worked, but while I
was feeling better, I wasn't yet well. The images had-
n't disappeared, and, as I now admitted, had been
overwhelming when I had returned alone to my
house.

We both knew things were worse than I was letting on to the group. He told me to think about it. It
was my choice, not anyone else's.

When I discussed it with Melissa, she thought it
was definitely the right thing to do this time and that
the job situation would resolve itself.

I made my decision. This wasn't giving in but
choosing, for once, to make things easier for myself. I
rang Felicity, a disconcertingly glamorous blonde
friend from uni, who'd always said that I was welcome
to stay with her when I was in town. She was delighted when I called, and said I could stay as long as I
liked.

'You know,' she added, 'I was wondering how you
were. I always worry when I haven't heard for a while.
Perth sounded like an odd choice, even for you.'

On the final day of the CBT course, Ray asked us how
we were all feeling about leaving.

I was nervous, and said so. I knew I'd be okay over the weekend, as Melissa was staying, but I was worried about afterwards.

When I told Ray that I wasn't ready to go home he was dismissive. I was just suffering a bit of anxiety which was perfectly normal. It wouldn't be any easier to leave if I stayed another week. He still thought I was doing the wrong thing by going back to Sydney. This wasn't the way the course was supposed to end. I was supposed to stay in touch with the other patients and report for follow-up group sessions. I was breaking the rules. It was evident that he also wasn't pleased that my psychiatrist was supporting my decision.

I went home and Melissa and I spent the weekend doing ordinary, girlie things – going to the movies, shopping, and just hanging out. It felt like a very long time since I'd done that with someone else, and I'd forgotten that it could be fun. That it was different with other people. I'd tried to train myself to be content to be alone, not just occasionally, but most of the time. I hadn't been very successful.

On Sunday evening Melissa flew home and it was just me again.

Chapter Twenty-seven

At work on Monday morning, I wasn't able to concentrate on anything. My mind, filled with ugliness, was in turmoil. Over and over I said to myself, I can't do this, I can't do this, I can't do this, I can't do this. It wasn't an affirmation that Ray would have approved of but I didn't care. I didn't care about coping strategies, negative self-talk, or anything else I'd learnt in the last two weeks: all I knew was that I shouldn't be at the office and that I couldn't be at home.

At 10.30 am I rang Dr P. He had half an hour available at lunchtime.

'I can't do it. I can't cope,' I said in tears again in his room.

He suggested another week in hospital might be a good idea.

My boss, who I'd always found a little intimidating, looked concerned when I said I'd come back too early. When I had first told her I was going into hospital, she'd asked which one. 'I don't really want to go into it,' I'd said, aware that the clinic was well known – only known – as a psychiatric hospital. I'd given her Annie's number should she need to get in touch.

'You don't look well,' she'd said, as I sat in her office that afternoon. 'Is another week really going to be enough?'

This was the time to tell her. 'Not really, but it's a bit complicated. I think – and my doctor agrees – that I'd be better going back east. This isn't something that is just going to go away.' There was a silence, and it became clear that I was going to have to tell her the truth. 'It's not terminal – just inconvenient.' I didn't know whether she would understand but decided it didn't matter.

I told her about the depression and the hospital. It was too much to explain about the thoughts, so I just said that I was having trouble with them. She could interpret this however she chose.

What I didn't expect was sympathy. 'I'm really sorry that things have been so difficult,' she said. She had a cousin with the same problem. He had a good job, great family and was great fun. She sighed. He had been hospitalised a number of times, for both mania and depression. 'I can understand why you didn't say anything. He doesn't talk about it either.'

We were both silent for a moment. I didn't know what to say.

She then moved on to more practical matters. 'When do you think you'll go?'

I said in a month or so. No longer.

The final week in hospital, while not as highly struc-tured as the first two, was still busy. There were other group therapy sessions I was encouraged to attend, on relationships and coping with day-to-day life. After the intensive CBT program they felt too easy, and they were also less intimate. Patients didn't have a chance to form any kind of bond, which meant that often, they just didn't care.

When they asked why I was there, I didn't have to think about my answer. 'Not cutting myself was driving me nuts.'

A small, pixie-faced woman, looked at my forearm, and then said dismissively, 'You've done it before: it's not like you do it to kill yourself, do you?' She was bitter. 'I overdosed and unfortunately my husband found me before the pills worked. Wanting to cut yourself is nothing. Nothing.'

It was a line I'd heard before, and one that really went to the heart of the matter. I too had struggled with the idea that wanting to cut myself was nothing – but it wasn't. It had almost destroyed me. But if even I found it difficult to understand, how could I expect anyone else to? One of the reasons that the bipolar diagnosis had appealed was that people understood it. I knew it didn't cover all my problems but it explained enough.

I'd met a man several years before. He was in his mid-thirties, gorgeous looking in a sharp-featured, Ralph Fiennes sort of way, and a successful corporate solicitor. One day he started having chest pains and breathing difficulties. Initially fearing a heart attack, he'd seen various specialists but after a number of tests, they told him that it wasn't a physical problem but a psychological one. He was suffering from panic attacks. By the time I knew him, he'd been forced to admit himself to hospital in order to sort them out and was acutely embarrassed about the condition. He hadn't ever thought that kind of thing would happen to him, and he didn't understand it. Didn't understand how it could have happened – and didn't want anyone to know. I got the feeling that he would have been happier if he really had had a heart problem.

I knew how he felt.

I understood that need for something tangible. Sometimes, when I was in hospital I looked at the other patients and felt inadequate. As though I hadn't done enough damage, didn't have enough scars. If I'd been really sick, I sometimes told myself, I would have had more. Then perhaps people would believe that it wasn't just a matter of pulling myself together.

It was only in Perth that I came to understand that my problem had ceased to be about cutting long ago. My real problem was about not cutting. If I had given in to myself, if I still used a razor, I wouldn't have been tormented.

It really was not cutting that had been driving me mad.

Not cutting, and trying to ignore it.

That week after the CBT program, I began to put into practice some of the techniques I'd learnt, but not all. Many aspects of the program still seemed too simplistic to bother with. I didn't, for instance, keep a mood diary with details about how I felt at certain times of the day. I knew my mood varied – I didn't need written proof. We'd also been encouraged to treat ourselves to special things, to take time out for ourselves. This was something else I didn't do: I found the idea of self-nurturing too close to the idea of self-indulgence, so wasn't comfortable with it. Besides, I lived alone, so wasn't everything I did for me?

I knew there were valid reasons that we were asked to do these things, I'd even written them down in my notes, but that didn't mean I was going to do them.

The one thing I really focused on, because I'd been so surprised to find that it even existed, was continuing to try to counteract my internal critic. Every time I noticed that little – or, to be honest, not so little – voice saying something negative I'd stop and think about it. Did it make sense? Did it really reflect what had happened? Did it reflect what I'd done? Was it, in CBT-speak, an example of black and white thinking, or over-generalisation?

If, for example, I forgot something, it didn't mean that I was stupid – even if that's what I automatically told myself – but only that I'd forgotten something. It didn't really reflect on me. If I said something foolish, it didn't mean I was an idiot, only that I'd said something foolish. It was the kind of thing that should be taught in Parenting 101, but often isn't – or is forgotten by the time children are old enough to go to school. Initially the process felt silly but as an experiment I kept at it.

Telling myself I was terrific wouldn't ever have worked but it seemed that I could do something about these small, disparaging thoughts.

Very quickly, as I began to listen to them, I realised that they weren't small at all.

It was like watching a film in which the narrator judges the protagonist's every action. From the very beginning, you know that the narrator hates that char-

acter and isn't going to let them get away with anything.

As I began to address the criticism, slowly, slowly,
something else began to happen. The images lessened.
The layers and layers of poisonous criticism had clearly, by making me feel inadequate and guilty, made the
images much worse, much more violent.

At first there would be hours without thoughts of
self-harm, and then I found it could be a whole afternoon. It was as though, after years of hostile occupa-
tion, I was getting my mind back – and the more of it
I had back, the more control I had. Because I wasn't
overwhelmed, I also began to be able to combat individual images by literally saying 'no' to myself when
they arrived. I was able to refuse to look at the screen.

Gradually, the images became less graphic, and the
traumatic, confronting pictures of slashed arms with
torrents of blood gave way to images of the back of my
wrists. The damage that I knew existed on the inside
was hidden from view.

Something had at last shifted and made it possible
for me to begin to protect myself.

As the assaults on my mind lessened, and I was able to
begin untangling what was happening, it became possible to see that the images really weren't random but
were in response to very specific thoughts, actions and
feelings. Something as simple as paying my rent a day
late could provoke, indirectly, the internal suggestion
that I slash my wrist. I was guilty. Bad. Cutting myself
was, the internal critic suggested, an appropriate
response to my behaviour.

It wasn't always about significant issues then, which explains why the problem had become so pervasive – and invasive. Those internal horror films were my way of appeasing myself, my critical self. If real blood wasn't going to flow, my mind had decided, the imaginary would have to do. It wasn't only an escape or a way of subverting my feelings, but imaginary punishment. And the imagination, as I had learnt over the years, is a very powerful thing.

Even if I managed to stop making myself feel so awful, there was no doubt that from time to time, life would make sure I felt rotten. That's how things work. I didn't know what I'd do instead of attempting to harm myself, how else I'd cope, and didn't think about it. It was enough, for the moment, to be feeling as though I were gaining some control. There were options that didn't involve drinking, smoking, drugs or obsessive behaviour. In the film *Secretary* the woman exchanges her sewing kit of blades for the pleasure of being spanked by James Spader. I was uncomfortable with being touched – except when I was drunk – so this wasn't really an option for me. But it wasn't just about being spanked. Like my friend Annabel, who had recently found God and as a direct result stopped cutting herself, the woman wanted someone else to take responsibility for her life. It was about submission, and while I could see the appeal, this wasn't what I wanted. There had to be another way.

My last month in Perth was unusually social. Melissa had left, but a friend who I hadn't seen for a very long time rang, saying she and her boyfriend would be in town for a few days. The timing was perfect. She'd rung on the weekend I'd been out of hospital, and they arrived three days after I'd been released the second time. I'd been there a month altogether.

I just had enough time to tidy, clean, and stock the fridge.

Work no longer mattered. I tidied files and put things in order, but did little that was constructive. My assistant, and the other women I worked with, were friendlier than they'd ever been. For the first time since I arrived, we began eating lunch together outside in the sun, rather than over papers at our desks. As we chatted, all three of them admitted that they thought things must have been difficult for me, but that as I'd seemed to be getting on well, they'd left me alone.

My boss offered to have me stay, if I felt that would help. She had a large house, and as her daughter was away at university there was a spare room, with its own bathroom and study. I didn't expect so much kindness, and like Melissa's spontaneous offer to come over when she heard I was sick, it made me feel uncomfortable. And sad somehow. There were people out there who cared, not because they had to but because they just did.

Annie and Charles asked me to dinner regularly, and to the movies. I still hadn't told them the truth about why I'd come over in the first place and why I was moving back, and they didn't ask.

Rachael, who I'd lived with in Melbourne, arrived after my other friends left. She'd been meaning to visit since I'd moved to Western Australia but my hospital visit, and imminent departure, propelled her into action. As I stood at the arrival gates at the airport terminal, it occurred to me that I was really looking forward to seeing her – and that I'd really enjoyed having other people to stay too.

I must be feeling better, I thought.

I could have told Rachael about Eva and the situation at the magazine when I lived in Melbourne – she would have been sympathetic, she would have understood. But then, the need for secrecy had seemed more important than anything else. I'd believed it was Eva's secret – open secret though it was – not mine, so hadn't talked about it.

If I'd known back then that talking didn't always mean betrayal, I might not have had to leave.

At 3 pm the day before the removalists arrived, and the day before I was due to fly back to Sydney, I started packing. Rachael had put the books in boxes but I hadn't realised that I had so many other things. By five I was struggling with a headache and the reali-sation that it was going to take all night. And then Annie rang.

She'd offered to help before but, old habits being hard to break, I'd said no.

I didn't even think about refusing this time, and she turned up half an hour later.

The six months in Perth had been worth it. It seemed that finally, I'd found the help I needed – and so now was able to accept the help I wanted.

Chapter Twenty-eight

By my bed was a parcel with a card on it. 'Dear Vic, Welcome back! Love Felicity.' Opening it, I found some expensive hand cream, the sort of thing that I'd never buy myself. As I unscrewed the top and smelt it, I thought, why not? Why didn't I buy this kind of thing? Was it self-indulgence if it made you happy? And did it matter if it was?

Now that I was back in Sydney I had no real plans, except to take things quietly. Felicity said again that I could stay as long as I liked and that she was glad to have the company.

Peter had paid off my credit card debt. Initially I'd said no to this, but over about a week he'd talked me into it. 'It's not a present, it's a loan.' It meant that I didn't have to take the first job I was offered, which was a very good thing. I was feeling better but fragile. Peter had always been generous, and I couldn't understand why he put himself out for me. Suddenly, I wanted to know.

'Did it ever upset you?' I asked. 'The razor blades, the hospitals?' He had always seemed impervious –

except for that occasion when he nearly fainted as I was being stitched up. It had made it easier for me to lean on him.

'Yes, yes it did.' He looked away.

Late one night, years before, after collecting yet another set of blades from me, he hadn't gone straight home. Instead, he walked into the middle of a nearby oval and cried. 'It could have been me.' Whatever I was struggling with, he had recognised it in himself.

Without any pressing debt, I looked forward to not working for a while, to sitting in cafés and reading, to visiting galleries, to catching up with friends. To enjoying myself.

On the second day back, I heard about a part-time job with a publishing company. It sounded interesting and although I didn't really want to rush into work, commonsense got the better of me. Vacancies in the industry didn't come up often.

After half an hour, the man on the other end of the phone asked me to come in and see him.

A week later, I turned up at the interview without feeling nervous. I didn't need the job, so there was no pressure. They wanted someone two or three days a week, and the hours were flexible. Initially, it would be for three months, while they decided what to do with the position. This wasn't permanent, but if I wanted to start on Monday, they'd be delighted.

I was stunned. The phone conversation had apparently been the real interview, the meeting a formality. The job was ideal as I could earn some money and at the same time think about what I wanted to do. Where I wanted to be.

For once there was no pressure on any front.

But I knew it wouldn't stay that way, so on the recommendation of Dr P, started seeing a new psychiatrist, Dr K. A small, plump man, he seemed more nervous than I was.

At the end of our first appointment he suggested that I needed twice-weekly psychotherapy. We could have a trial period of a month or so, and see how it went. The idea was that I would establish a relationship with him that could be a model for others, a relationship in which I could feel comfortable expressing myself. He seemed to think that this was a big problem for me and that it made me feel more isolated. It was strange to be in a psychiatrist's office and not talking about the images or the urges or depression. Relationships, isolation – they seemed so mundane somehow. I wasn't sure that we needed to talk about these things, but, out of a sense of obligation, I continued to visit him.

The truth was that things were changing. And while isolation had sounded mundane, I noticed that once I began to let people help me, I felt better and it wasn't so much because they were helping me, but because I was letting them. And it made them happy. Felicity said she liked having someone to come home to and have dinner with, someone to chat to.

There wasn't anything wrong with needing other people. It was normal.

The job, which I'd been a little unsure about, was great. I could use all the skills I'd learnt previously but no-one expected me to know everything. And I was enjoying working three days a week.

After two months, they began interviewing people for the permanent position, people who had experience in the area. I wasn't sure what to do, as I wanted to stay but didn't feel confident. I approached the man who'd hired me originally, and asked his advice. There were lots of things we could do to improve the way the area was run. I hadn't suggested much so far, but would love the opportunity to make some changes. Was it worth even applying?

He looked surprised. Did I want to work full time?

I didn't even need to think about it: I'd had a break and it was time to get back into it. I put in an application and waited.

Waiting wasn't something I was good at and the strain began to affect me. Violent images fluttered through my head. They were nothing to do with criti-cal thoughts but were a direct response to stress. The only response I knew. But it wasn't just the wait that was causing these bloody pictures to reappear.

Eva had commissioned a review from me, and it was overdue. I'd put off calling her to ask for an extension but finally picked up the phone. The assistant editor answered. 'Vic, we've been trying to contact you.' Of course they had, I should have rung a week ago. 'Eva died yesterday.'

Before I knew what I was saying it came out, 'She didn't...?'

'No, she died of a heart attack. We just wanted to tell you personally, because she was so fond of you.'

The last time I'd seen her she'd seemed so much better. She'd put on weight, and although she blamed the medication, she looked healthy for the first time in years. We had sat in the same Italian restaurant and had drunk too much chardonnay, as we'd done so many times before, and the manager had greeted us both like members of the family. Where had I been? What had I been doing? I was asked. Eva's hands were free from bandages, and she told me that she'd been seeing a psychiatrist twice a week for several years now. He had been encouraging her to write.

Would it be sensible to publish something? she'd asked. We'd then talked about the taboo involving self-mutilation, and the pros and cons of writing about it. Perhaps a book would help families and friends understand what we went through, what was going on in our heads. What we couldn't tell them. There were risks, of course. Did she want people knowing about her private life? Was she prepared to talk about it, on the radio, in the media? And what if instead of helping, it made someone start doing it?

She needed to weigh it up but I, for one, hoped she'd write something. There were handbooks and memoirs around about anorexia, bulimia, depression, and so many other disorders, but very little was available on self-harm. There was plenty on the Web, but it was often too graphic, or too clinical. I knew this because I'd tried many times to find something.

As I sat on the train home that evening, I wondered what had happened to what she'd written, and indeed what her story was. What made someone so clever, so able, so caring, harm herself?

Was her story, in essence, so very different from mine?

There was to be a memorial service at the end of the week, and I decided to fly down to Melbourne for the day.

The service was moving, and the wake filled with all of the people I remembered from my time at the magazine. There were authors, academics, newspaper editors, and critics. After a couple of hours, it was time to say goodbye to various people.

'You know that there has already been speculation about who'll take over?' one asked.

It wasn't something I'd thought about, and was surprised that he'd even mentioned it. But then, he was a part of the company that ran the magazine, and it was his job to think about succession. My name had come up in discussion – was I committed to Sydney, and what I was doing now? The position was about to be advertised but would I think about it?

I didn't know what to say.

'Eva couldn't speak highly enough of you.'

On the plane home, I didn't know what to think. I'd always wanted to edit a magazine – specifically that magazine – but Eva had always said she planned to die in the job. I didn't think she'd meant it quite so literally.

I was delighted, amazed, flattered, that other people thought it was something I could do. And I knew they were right. I knew the systems, the writers, the printers. It would mean moving back to Melbourne but my furniture was still in storage, so that wouldn't be hard. There'd be competition, I knew that, it was being advertised after all, but I was in with a strong chance. They'd actually asked me to apply.

I kept the conversation to myself.

Two days later, on the way to see my new psychiatrist, I had one of the worst mental images I'd ever had. In the past, they'd operated like film screenings, and while they'd been awful, they hadn't taken up my whole mind. This was how I'd managed to continue doing other things, like talking, or driving. This was different. I felt as though I'd been hit. Both my arms were in front of me, covered in open, gaping wounds with blood flowing freely from them. I was enveloped.

I told Dr K.

He asked what I thought might have caused it.

'I don't know, I don't know.' Things were going well. There was a possibility of what I'd always thought of as a dream job, and I was still in the running for the full-time position where I was, which I was really enjoying. I didn't understand what was happening.

He asked if I was worried about anything.

'No,' I said, and told him about the funeral, and the magazine.

'Do you actually want the job in Melbourne, were they to offer it to you?'

I was taken aback. Of course I wanted it, I'd always wanted it. Or did I? Or was it that I felt I should want it because it was prestigious and would be a great career move, because it would be challenging, stimulating and high profile. Because someone else thought I should have it.

I'd not admitted to myself that the past associations worried me, and that I was worried about how demanding the job would be. Deep down I knew that even though I could do it, Eva's shoes would be very hard to fill. I wasn't sure that I was the right one to try.

Over the last two months, I'd been happy. Work was satisfying and not stressful, my friends were close by, and, I had to admit, I loved the weather and the harbour. Did I want to give that up? Would it be sensible?

That night I called the person who'd spoken to me at the wake and told him I wouldn't be applying. This was after ringing previously to say I would. As I put the phone down I wondered if I'd done the right thing, and indeed if the job at the magazine would have really been offered to me.

I'd never find out, and perhaps that was a good thing.

Over the next couple of days I began to feel calmer again, and on the following Monday, I was offered my job, permanently.

It was time to get my own place again. This time, I wanted it to be cosy, a place where I wanted to spend time. I found an art deco one-bedroom flat with big windows and the harbour at the end of the street. I bought bookcases, wooden blinds and seagrass mats. I hung pictures and bought saucepans. For the first time, it didn't feel as though I were camping. I stopped sitting on the edge of my chair.

At around seven one Sunday evening I heard a knock on the door. I wasn't expecting anyone and thought that perhaps it was a neighbour. It was Alex. He looked the same as ever.

He was just passing by apparently, and thought he'd say hello. He'd been meaning to for a while.

I'd deliberately not called him since getting back.

He asked if I'd had dinner.

I wasn't sure if it was a general question, or if he was suggesting we go out. As ever, it was hard to tell. I said no, and offered him soup, which was what I'd been planning to have.

He made a face. 'No, thanks. There must be somewhere decent around here.'

So he was asking me out.

I was wearing an old T-shirt and shorts. 'There is, but do you mind if I don't change?' I didn't want him to think he was worth making an effort for.

'God no, I don't care.' He never had.

We were the only customers in the restaurant, so the waiters hovered. After ordering wine, he filled me in on what he'd been up to recently. Things seemed to be going well for him too and he'd just been offered a job overseas. We talked, and ate, and drank, and actually enjoyed ourselves. It had taken ten years to get to this point.

I still wondered what he was doing there.

As we walked home it became obvious. He was single and wanted what he'd always wanted from me. Only this time it was different. I wasn't interested and I said no. He could sleep on the couch if he wanted, but not with me.

He went home.

Epilogue

The job is terrific, though it does get stressful some-times. I'm much better at handling this now but still find, if I'm not careful, that my mind will misbehave, and I find myself shaking my head, saying 'no', active-ly getting rid of anything disturbing, unwanted and unhelpful.

I think about what a friend of mine once said in regard to work: keep what happens in proportion, after all, 'nobody dies'. And I try to take my father's zen-like advice and just let stress, in whatever form, wash over me. Mostly I just enjoy what I do, and when I'm not concentrating on work, I think about what I want for lunch, who I want to visit on the weekend, or what movie I want to see next. Ordinary things.

'My mother was horrified by the idea that I was having a book published about my experience of self harm, and very upset once she read it. It is the kind of book no mother wants their daughter to write, as no mother wants her daughter to have gone through it. That said, it has meant that finally, after years of tip-toeing around the subject, we have been able to talk about what happened. And talk about it honestly. As a result, we now have a better relationship than we have had for many years.

My father is very proud that I have done it, and has been quietly supportive throughout the writing, even though he knew that the content would be disturbing.'

Melissa and Archie read the first draft. Archie said that he had no idea. No idea. And that he wasn't mentioned much, was he?

Jeremy doesn't know about it. When he does he'll be annoyed that he's mentioned even less.

Alex knows, and agrees that we'll each see things in a different way. Memory is like that. He's not concerned.

I still take a mood stabiliser, Tegretol, and see a psychiatrist about once a year, but otherwise that's it. It's really only my long-time friends and family who have any idea about my past these days, as it's normally not something I talk about. Mostly, I don't need to.

A year ago, late one night after a work dinner, my boss noticed my scars, which are faded now. 'Are they what they look like?' she asked.

I thought for a moment. 'I guess so, yes. I went through a bit of a tough time.'

'Good on you for getting through it.' She's not mentioned the matter again. And though I wear short sleeves in summer, no-one else at work has mentioned it.

Although it's now six years since I last picked up a razor blade, I'm still acutely conscious of the damage I did. I can't be otherwise; whenever I shower, pick up something, shake hands with someone or even lie in bed at night with a book, I can see the scars. Sometimes I pull the sheet up so as not to be reminded but really, there's no way I'm going to be able to forget what I did. And thought. But maybe that's no bad thing. It's a warning against complacency, as well as being a constant reminder of how much better things can be.

Author's Note

The names and some details have been changed to protect other people's privacy. I think it is also important to point out that this book is not meant to represent the experiences or views of anyone else. This is my story, told as I remember it. I'm not speaking on behalf of other people who self harm, or the medical profession. The disorder varies widely in severity, and I understand cognitive behaviour therapy isn't a conventional treatment for it.

My last visit was to a psychiatrist about six months ago and we discussed the issue of diagnosis. He suggested that I suffered from bipolar 2, which is similar to bipolar 1, but not as severe. He advised me to continue taking my medication.

I can also understand why there are so few books written about self harm by sufferers: they are damn hard to write.

Acknowledgements

I'd like to thank all those friends who have been so encouraging over the last eighteen months while I've been writing, and this group includes one of my favourite people. He didn't know what the book was about but constantly reassured me that whatever I produced would be wonderful.

I'd also like to thank my family, in particular my older brother and sister-in-law, who listened to me talk about myself and didn't once roll their eyes when I started to say, again, that perhaps I'd change the structure. They've both been unfailingly supportive.

All at Allen & Unwin have been great from the start, especially Jo Paul, Rebecca Kaiser, April Murdoch, Marie Baird and Patrick Gallagher.

And finally, I'd like to thank the GP and psychiatrist in Perth who finally got it right.

Helplines and Information Resources

Samaritans
24 hour, free helpline.
08457 90 90 90
www.samaritans.org/know/selfharm/

The National Self Harming Network
Support for self harmers from those who have experienced self harm to themselves or seen it in family and friends.
NSHN
PO Box 7264
Nottingham, NG1 6WJ
www.nshn.co.uk

The Self Harm Alliance
Self harmers helpline. Open Tuesday 6-7pm,
Thursday 11am – 1pm, Sunday 6-7pm.
01242 578 820
www.selfharmalliance.co.uk

MIND infoline
Information on a range of issues including self-harm.
08457 660 163

Self-harm Information Resource
Information website about self-harm.
www.selfharm.org.uk

Young Minds
Provides help for parents and others with concerns
about the mental health of a child or young person.
0800 018 2138

The Eating Disorders Association
Helpline providing support and information on all
types of eating disorders. Open Monday to Friday
8.30am-8.30pm. Saturday 1pm-4.30pm.
www.edauk.com

The National Centre for Eating Disorders
Information website.
www.eating-disorders.org.uk

The Acne Support Group
Helpline providing support and information on acne
and other skin conditions.
0870 870 2263